THE GHOST ROCKETS

THE GHOST ROCKETS

MYSTERY MISSILES AND PHANTOM PROJECTILES IN OUR SKIES

MICAH HANKS

ROCKETEER PRESS ❧ NORTH CAROLINA

The Ghost Rockets
Edited by Tyler Pittman and Alex Hanks
Cover Design by Scott Roberts
Printed in the U.S.A.

For more information, or to order additional copies of this title, please visit www.micahhanks.com or email info@micahhanks.com.

ROCKETEER
PRESS

P.O. Box 884
Enka, NC 28728

For my grandmother Lucille, who always encouraged me to find the answers, and to forge my own path; and for granddad William, the first war historian to ever tell me about Ghost Rockets and Foo Fighters... all my respect, admiration, and love goes to the two of you. May you both be blessed, always.

Acknowledgements

There are many whose hard work and persistence in searching for answers to the UFO mystery over the years became instrumental to the completion of this book: Peter Davenport of the National UFO Reporting Center, for all of his patience and dedication to unraveling the impossible; Mack Maloney, for his friendship, and for continuing to shed light on the military and wartime component to all of this; Peter Robbins, whose kindness and persistence are an inspiration to us all; Scott Alan Roberts, who despite not labeling himself a UFO researcher, manages to see through the hubris and stagnation in this field; Richard Dolan for his friendship, humor, and his timeless contributions to the study of unexplained aerial phenomenon; Race Hobbs for helping facilitate a cohesive network of researchers that functions more like family than a group of associates; to my brother Caleb Hanks, and to Tyler Pittman, each for their many contributions to our various endeavors and research; Abigail Roberts for enduring hours at a time with me during the completion of this project; the pioneers at NASA who have spent the last several decades forging a path for mankind into the outer cosmos; and finally, my sincere thanks and appreciation to James, who fills yet another shadowy gap in this strange ongoing narrative with his consistent insight and knowledge.

A man, as they say, is only as good as those with whom he surrounds himself; with that in mind, I may be the very best, and I'm grateful for all of it, and for all of you.

CONTENTS

Introduction

One: Apparitions Over the Earth

Two: Ghost Rockets in the Atomic Age

Three: The Mystery Missiles: Cold War and Cover Ups

Four: Fear and Flares Over Long Island

Five: NASA and the New Millennium

Six: Conclusions: Firing Beyond the Lunatic Fringe

Appendix: A Chronological Listing of Ghost Rocket Sightings from 1942 to the Present

Notes

Index

Suggested Reading

About the Author

INTRODUCTION

In December of 2009, observers across the northern-most regions of Scandinavia were treated to a spectacular aerial display, as a bright blue cloud of flame twisted its way through the sky. Photographs of the unusual phenomenon were carried by a number of news agencies, and observers began to speculate as to what the strange object could have been. Had an extraterrestrial spacecraft streaked through the skies over Norway?

Paal Brekke was one of those observers who, in the hours after the object appeared, had begun to closely examine pictures and video taken of the object. As a senior adviser at the Norwegian Space Centre, Brekke and his colleagues were of the opinion that this object, while extraordinary looking, had indeed been terrestrial in origin: the likely culprit had been a failed missile test launch. This was later confirmed by authorities with the Russian Defense Ministry, who acknowledged that a Bulava ballistic missile had failed shortly after launching from a submarine in the White Sea. [1]

Less than one year later, an event that was far less bizarre in appearance nonetheless managed to cause heated speculation regarding an unidentified object which, as it passed over California, led some to believe that a similar missile-like-object had been fired from the California coast. On Monday, November 8, 2010, a television news helicopter documented the apparent projectile as it streaked across the sky, leaving a glowing orange contrail illuminated by the Pacific sunset.

Military officials were slow to respond to the incident as area news teams scrambled to obtain statements regarding the nature and origin of the object. Incidentally, a Delta II rocket had been launched from nearby Vandenberg Air Force Base, which carried an Italian satellite into orbit just three days earlier. However, no subsequent launches could be confirmed from Vandenberg, or any other locations in the area. Further intrigue was raised after a televised statement by Robert Ellsworth, a former Deputy Secretary of Defense and U.S. Ambassador to NATO, who described it as "spectacular," and that it even might have been, "a missile test timed as a demonstration of American military might," planned to coincide with President Barack Obama's concurrent tour of Asia. [2]

There were less enthusiastic interpretations of the California "mystery missile," which included the idea that, instead of an American show of military strength, perhaps some other nation—namely China—had sought to do the same. However, within a few days, and following careful review of the available data, a Defense Department spokesman named David Lapan announced that he and others in officialdom were now satisfied with a more conventional explanation for the object. By all accounts, there had been no missiles fired around the time, and the object in question had merely been a passenger jet whose vapor trail, illuminated by the setting sun, had taken on an unordinary, and perhaps a bit *extraordinary*, appearance. [3]

The main difference between the missile scare over California and the Norwegian incident a year earlier had been that in the latter instance, the object seen over Europe actually *had* been a missile. Regardless, both were misinterpreted at the outset as being something out-of-place, or perhaps even anomalous, when in fact there were very common explanations behind these occurrences. And yet, the Norwegian missile story nonetheless continued to draw controversy in 2013, when science writer Phillip Plait featured it amidst a roundup of rather easily debunked UFOs for his article in the March issue of *Astronomy Magazine*. Skeptics like Plait would look at the story as one of many cases where presumed "UFO believers" had leapt at an otherworldly explanation before all the facts had been taken into consideration. In contrast to Plait's assertion, however, much of the UFO community instead balked at the idea that such a widely reported missile incident had been used to support an anti-UFO argument.

Missiles, after all, just aren't the kind of aircraft that are typically viewed as being anomalous in nature. In the case of the Norwegian aerial spiral, a strange looking exhaust trail from a failed rocket led to a display in the sky so unusual that it had *appeared* otherworldly to some observers; indeed, to the untrained eye, it may even have looked like a UFO. Aside from this, there was nothing particularly strange about the case; the same could be said of the misidentified aircraft over California one year later that sparked so much controversy.

However, on a few occasions there have been stories of missiles of unknown origin that have cropped up over the years, which also managed to do a better job in terms of keeping us guessing. For instance, late in the afternoon on Monday, January 25, 2010, Darlene Stewart, a resident of Harbour Mille, Newfoundland, had gone outside to photograph the sunset. It was a clear evening, and as she readied her camera, Stewart was startled to see a large, metallic object flying through the sky overhead. She began to photograph the strange craft, and the resulting pictures clearly show what appears to be a large missile in flight, producing a luminous vapor trail behind it.

Another Harbour Mille resident, Emmy Pardy, said the object had been "grey and silver in colour," and that it, "looked like an oversized bullet with a trail of fire behind it." The objects moved silently through the sky, and remained visible for approximately fifteen minutes. According to Pardy, an officer with the Royal Canadian Mounted Police apparently confirmed to her over the course of two follow-up calls that the objects had indeed been missiles, which were launched from Saint Pierre-Miquelon, a territory nearby under French occupation. However, the Canadian government later denied the missile allegations, stating that there had never been evidence of any missiles being fired, and further ruling out the possibility that hobbyists in the region had been firing rockets. [4] If such theories could be ruled out, then what was the object Darlene Stewart managed to photograph, which was emblazoned across not just the sky, but also several newspapers and websites? Quite obviously, *something* had been seen, but it was also apparently something officialdom preferred not to have to acknowledge or speak about.

There are a number of other missile-related incidents that, while largely unknown to the general public, remain even more curious and tantalizing than any of the aforementioned. Many of these cases, which were investigated, or even *reported,* by trained airline pilots and others with expertise in the fields of aviation and ballistics, seemed to involve actual projectiles, rather than the simple misidentification of various objects or natural phenomena. While many researchers who take interest in unidentified flying objects become easily enthralled with the more exotic sounding cases in the available literature, claims of encounters that involve these "mystery" missiles represent, at times, an equally unexplainable—and yet remarkably persistent—element within the catalogue of anomalous terrestrial activity. In other words, the technology being observed often appears mysterious, but still of *earthly* origin. And of course, objects appearing so similar in design to military projectiles would seem to represent a variety of phenomenon that poses a serious, and potentially deadly threat to the civilian populous as well.

Why, then, are these reports so easily ignored or dismissed in official channels? It so often seems the case that when an explanation seems *impossible*, people will react with dismissal. Thus, many would treat the idea of exotic aerial vehicles in our skies as absurd; much the same, if no immediate explanation presents itself for why a commercial airline pilot witnessed a missile coasting along at high speeds as he flew over the Americas, the incident is hardly given a second thought, let alone taken seriously.

And yet, the mysterious presence of missiles and rockets in our skies predates some of the earliest and most famous modern UFO reports. Strange projectiles, known today as "ghost rockets," were reportedly seen throughout the skies over Sweden and various other parts of Europe immediately following World War II. The common belief at the time had been that these objects represented Russian tests with captured German technology, such as the infamous V-2 rockets, the first short-range ballistic missiles developed by the Nazis for use against Europe during the conflict. It would later be determined that Russia, at the time, had not possessed any rocket propulsion technology sophisticated enough to account for the curious projectiles reported over Europe after the war; and yet, many credible reports of rockets and similar looking flying objects, as well as the smoke trails they left behind them, were reported during this period. [5]

For many, it would only seem logical that reports of rockets would persist throughout the years immediately following World War II. After all, while the primary conflict was over, the major emerging superpowers were left uncertain as to just how much recovered technology their adversaries might possess. Only with the passing of the years would it finally become obvious that historical knowledge could not fully account for the anomalous appearances of missiles and projectiles in the skies above us, evidence for which this essay will seek to examine more thoroughly, in a unique and largely overlooked sub-plot that has carried out virtually unnoticed in its relation to conventional views toward avionics, as well as other anomalous aerial phenomena.

My inquiry into the strange nature of "anomalous missile" reports began in early May 2013, when a story out of Scotland alleged that a passenger jet and its crew had barely missed a collision with a "UFO" over Baillieston in December of 2012.

The story detailed how an Airbus A320 traveling over Scotland had apparently come within a mere 300 feet of a large blue and silver object, while on final approach to Glasgow airport. The object passed beneath the aircraft quickly enough that the pilots hadn't been able to react, prompting a report of the incident, filed afterward with the UK Airprox Board, to describe the incident as having been a high-risk for collision. Further investigation ruled out the possibility that the object had been another aircraft, or any kind of meteorological balloon operating in the area. [6]

It was initially reported that devices ranging from the plane's onboard traffic collision avoidance system, to radar at Glasgow Air Traffic Control, had been unable to track the object. However, approximately 1.3 miles east of the incoming Airbus A320, radar operators at Prestwick Air Traffic Control did report later that they observed a mysterious radar track in the area, representing an aircraft or object they could not account for.

It soon became evident, however, that Billy Orsmond, an area schoolboy, had reportedly lost control of "a 6ft-long helium-filled shark toy and watched it fly into the air, never to be seen again." According to Orsmond's father, the object described by pilots of the Airbus A320 was a perfect match for the shark toy, which the senior Orsmond notes had been used by his son to torment and terrify his mother, paired with other general mischief-making endeavors. None would manage to top the events following the shark's "escape" in December, which led pilots aboard the plane to question whether they had seen a missile streaking along beneath them. [7]

While it seems unlikely now—if not impossible—that the object in this instance was a genuine projectile, the fact that early reports describe it as resembling a missile, and that it came dangerously close to the aircraft on approach to Glasgow, managed to capture my interest. Despite the prosaic explanation that emerged later, I became interested in seeing what other sorts of objects might have been witnessed by pilots over the years; would there be any precedent for the appearance of things that could be defined as *real* "missiles," or for that matter, any other variety of projectiles or anomalous aircraft seen by pilots that would arouse concern?

The May 5, 1991 edition of *The Sunday Times* detailed an incident that would soon become recurrent throughout my research into reports of projectile-like objects of unknown origin. The incident, which took place in 1982, almost a decade prior to publication in the *Times*, involved an Italian DC-9 aircraft that came dangerously close to colliding with an object at an altitude of close to 27,000 feet. However, unlike many missile reports I would find, the object seen in this instance actually *exploded*, and did so very close to the Italian passengers observing. Descriptions of the object prior to the blast entailed a "fast-moving projectile, like a missile" that had been observed. [8]

What I learned from studying reports like this truly amazed me; as a long-time researcher of aerial phenomenon, by now I am quite used to looking for commonplace explanations, often veiled by the mystique of unusual and circumstantial environmental factors, for things that seem wholly inexplicable at the outset. In many of the cases we will examine shortly, I cannot express ease in assuring the reader that what these reports entail will offer such simple explanations. It would be a stretch to assert that there is anything "paranormal" about the majority of the cases presented here; however, in many instances, we are left to ponder the implications of bizarre missile sightings and other incidents that have taken place within American airspace, as well as tales of similar projectile phenomenon that have occurred elsewhere in the world. If these were indeed projectiles of any kind, then many of the cases reviewed here would have had to represent a potential danger to those nearby. Some of the reported cases, which *did* turn deadly, would strongly suggest that if projectiles had been involved, there had been an effort to conceal that information from the public. But perhaps most troubling of all is the question of who, or what organization, might fire such projectiles, often well outside the jurisdictions of missile test sites? Finally, if they are indeed the result of some kind of operation most of us in the general public still know little of, what could their purpose be? Can all the appearances of anomalous missiles, or "ghost rockets" as they were often called after the rash of incidents that occurred in Scandinavia following the Second World War, really be chalked up to misidentifications, hoaxes, or the reliable old argument that "accidents just happen"?

Quite simply, there is obvious potential danger here; a grave concern that surrounds the appearance of projectiles for which no official explanations exist. In the end, you will be left to judge what the nature of these reports may entail, and whether such technologies are of concern to the public, or merely the stuff of the imagination. But one thing is clear: we cannot, at present, account for all the objects seen in our skies, based on information that is willingly provided to the public. In the truest sense, the reports that follow do involve unidentified flying objects, and while many are not likely to be of any exotic origin, they are certainly an element of the ongoing UFO mystery that must be examined and given serious consideration.

Chapter One

Apparitions Over the Earth

"For some weeks a fair number of 'ghost rockets' going from south-east to north-west have been reported from various parts of the eastern coast of Sweden. Eye witnesses say that they look like glowing balls and are followed by a tail of smoke more or less visible. So many reports cannot be put down to pure imagination in the matter. As there is no definite evidence that the phenomena are of meteoric origin, there is growing suspicion that they are a new kind of radio-controlled V-weapon on which experiments are carried out."

London Daily Telegraph, July 12, 1946

In an incident widely reported in UFO circles, Captain Jack Puckett, the assistant chief of flying safety, Tactical Air Command, was piloting a twin engine C-47 on August 1, 1946, when he observed one of the earliest American instances of what would later become known as "ghost rocket" phenomenon. Having left Langley Field and now on course for MacDill Air Force Base, situated just southwest of Tampa, Florida, he was approximately thirty miles from his destination when a brightly illuminated object, flying dangerously close to his C-47, nearly collided with him and his crew. "It continued toward us on a collision course, at our exact altitude," Puckett later wrote in an incident report. "At about 1,000 yards, it veered to cross our path. We observed it to be a long, cylindrical shape approximately twice the size of a B-29 bomber, with luminous portholes." Puckett and his company continued watching the object until it disappeared over the horizon, spanning a distance that Puckett judged to be as much as 100 miles, over the course of three minutes. This data would suggest that the aircraft had been moving twice the speed of sound, which, in 1946, no known aircraft possessed the ability to do. [1]

The object Puckett witnessed also produced a strange, sparkling tail, much like a rocket would; this detail would certainly present a lot of confusion among aviation officials at the time, in addition to increasing speculation about new kinds of technologies that might be under development elsewhere in the world. The technical information about rocketry advancements spearheaded in Nazi Germany during World War II, along with many of the leading experts in this field, were acquired by the British, Soviet, and American governments during and immediately following the war. America had previously gained access to V-2 rocket technology the Allies recovered at the Mittelbau-Dora concentration camp near Nordhausen, where an underground German rocket base known as the Mittelwerk factory, had been located. British forces managed to take away a wealth of information prior to the later Soviet occupation of the area. By late 1945, this information formed the basis of what became Operation Backfire, a program where British V-2 rockets were built and launched for purposes of demonstrating their capabilities.[2] The following year, a Soviet project called Operation Osoaviakhim would secure similar technical specifications about the German rocket programs, as well as personnel that were brought back to the Soviet Union, mirroring the Allied allocation of rocket scientists the likes of Wernher Von Braun to the United States. [3]

It is worth noting that while these newly launched rocket test programs were underway in the years following the war, a strange prominence of reports describing mysterious aircraft had also been taking place over Scandinavia, with Sweden being a central focus of the strange sightings. The objects were sometimes said to resemble rockets, although no official explanation had been given for who could be behind their operation, or why they would have been launched. In at least some instances, the mysterious craft being observed would bear similarity to Puckett's description of the strange "rocket" he saw over Florida in 1946, which seemed to possess characteristics that were similar both to experimental projectiles being tested at the time, as well as some variety of manned aircraft. However, history suggests that there was no convincing connection that existed between official rocket programs involving recovered German technology, and the reports of these strange new objects, whose mysterious appearances and aerial acrobatics led to their being dubbed, for lack of any better term, "ghost rockets."

THE ROCKET WAVE BEGINS

A few of the earliest reports of anomalous rockets do have their origins during the actual war years. One incident, which transpired over Halberstadt, Germany on the night of January 2, 1944, involved the pilot of an RAF Mosquito who claimed that he and his navigator had observed a mysterious rocket that began to pursue them. The object had been moving "incredibly fast," and had apparently made a 90 degree turn at one point, aligning itself parallel to their path of flight, before vanishing suddenly. [4] Similar reports of rocket-like objects over Germany had been collected as early as 1942, though it remains unclear whether the objects seen in cases like this, while being reported as "rockets," had merely borrowed from the best conventional explanations at the time, or if it had actually resembled a rocket. Thus, in many cases it was supposed that these seemingly mysterious objects had been misidentified natural phenomena, such as meteors. On January 18, 1946, an American C-54 transport plane was flying over France late in the evening when the pilot reported seeing "a brilliant meteor" over the horizon. The object appeared only briefly, then vanished as it descended toward the Earth. However, to the pilot's surprise, the object then *reappeared,* and seemed to gain approximately one degree of altitude over the Eastern horizon before finally vanishing for good.

Many would argue that such an object could not have been a meteor, since it seemed to defy gravity, at least for a moment, during its brief reappearance. However, contrary to paranormal interpretations of what the underlying cause might be, there are actually many occasions where natural forces have caused meteors to behave strangely while entering Earth's atmosphere. American physicist William R. Corliss wrote that such "erratic meteors" can result from aerodynamic forces heating the rock as it falls toward the Earth, at which time "gases may be expelled which can initiate sharp course changes due to jet action." [5] Even today, such naturally occurring factors have no doubt continued to influence people's perception of alleged UFOs, as they did back in the late 1940s when fears regarding the use of newly attained rocket technologies had been particularly high.

It is worth noting here, however, that there are other instances where reports of so-called "erratic meteors" have simply been too strange to qualify for natural phenomenon. Going all the way back to the nineteenth century, on August

1, 1871 over Marseilles, France, an object described as a "very slow meteor" was observed traveling eastward, before stopping completely, and then hovering momentarily in the sky. Next it travelled north, stopped a second time, and then resumed traveling east again. The object was in view for a total of 20 minutes, and commenting on the strange object in his Sourcebook entry on "Erratic Meteors," Corliss notes that, "Such apparitions are probably not true meteors," and that similar reports have been categorized alongside what are called, "High-Level Nocturnal Lights, so-named in UFO literatures." [6]

The case to be made here is that, while many of the early reports of the post-war era refer to "ghost rockets," often the craft or objects being observed were either too vague in appearance, or perhaps were reported too vaguely by witnesses, to be accurately defined as projectiles. This truism has led a number of more skeptical researchers over the years to discount many reports emanating from the period, which have been attributed to hysteria or "war nerves" similar to that which inspired the 37th Coast Artillery Brigade to fire 1,400 anti-aircraft shells into the night air over Los Angeles on February 25, 1942. The incident, best-known today as the "Battle of Los Angeles," had likely been caused by meteorological balloons that were released in the area shortly before the presumed "attack." [7] Despite this, the story has seen wide circulation in UFO circles, and is believed by some to be a genuine incident involving an unidentified aircraft, which moved far too slowly to have been an enemy plane. Thus, one might argue that ghost rockets should be viewed with the same sort of skepticism, and stories of strange projectiles seen over Scandinavia, the Mediterranean, and parts of North Africa and the Americas were merely the artifacts of a social climate colored by paranoia at the time.

While this logic certainly does apply in many cases, perhaps we should not be too quick to prejudge all the wartime rocket reports, or those occurring shortly after the war, as spurious tales materialized from the indiscriminate filter of war-ravaged minds. By the same token, it would be wise to acknowledge what actually *was known* to be going on "behind the scenes" with officialdom, with particular respect toward the necessity for secrecy during such operations. History has shown that part of the Soviet desire to quietly remove German technology and personnel from their portions of occupied Germany had been to prevent the backlash that would be incurred by Allied forces, had they been made aware that certain actions had not been in compliance with Allied Control Council agreements at the time. Fortean researchers Jerome Clark and Loren Coleman made a similar observation in their 1975 book, *The Unidentified*:

> When the great post-war UFO wave broke, northern Europeans, still traumatized by memories of the horrors of rocket warfare... naturally assumed that the "ghost rockets" were foreign weapons. The UFOs for their part did little to allay such fears: most of them appeared out of the

southeast, from the direction of Peenemunde, now in Soviet hands. With Cold War paranoia already in full swing, Europe was rife with rumors about Stalin's intentions, and the Soviet refusal to allow the Allies to investigate persistent reports of war-material construction in the Russian zone contributed measurably to the growing uneasiness. The Swedish newspaper *Aftonbaldet* speculated that "Sweden is systematically being dotted in on a Russian artillery map... and is being used as an object of demonstration directed not to us but to the big world." [8]

Misdirection: Ghost Rockets and Secret Nazi Technologies

The controversy that inevitably surrounded the allotment of German rocket and propulsion technologies after the war would become famous for muddying the already darkened waters of the greater UFO mystery. Claims have been made over the years that rocket scientist Wernher von Braun, who went to work for the American Space Program, would later warn about counterintelligence programs and what, in essence, would amount to "false flag" operations, aimed at engineering public perceptions that UFOs were, in fact, extraterrestrial spacecraft. Similar misinformation alerts have been brought into question regarding von Braun's mentor, Hermann Oberth, who later became an outspoken advocate for an extraterrestrial theory

Oberth and von Braun studying orbital trajectories at the Army Ballistic Missile Agency in Huntsville, AL. © NASA, 1958. Source: Wikipedia

behind UFOs, and had even written an article on the subject that was featured in the May 1962 edition of *Fate Magazine*. The piece, "Dr. Hermann Oberth Discusses UFOs," is often referenced in relation to the scientist's views on the potential extraterrestrial component regarding reports of UFOs. However, alternative historian and con-spiracy researcher Joseph Farrell brought this piece into question in his 2012 book *Saucers, Swastikas, and Psyops*, citing it as evidence that Oberth's expressed opinions about UFOs could have actually been part of a misinformation operation. "The possibility arises that Dr. Oberth was being deliberately disingenuous in his remarks," Farrell argues, later submitting evidence for Oberth's involvement in a secret Nazi physics project known as *Die Glocke,* or "The

Bell," as it is famously called. The implication here is that an even deeper level of conspiracy pertaining to what technologies the Nazis had actually been working with may yet exist. [9]

I too will admit that there are elements of fact—and at times, compelling ones—which surround the modern fascination that has erupted around the so-called "Nazi UFO mythos." The entirety of this alternative historical view stems largely from the obvious innovations that occurred in Germany during the war years, and it could be said with almost certainty that this sort of information also had some bearing on the "ghost rocket" reports from immediately after the Second World War. However, in our modern Internet culture, researchers are all too often engaged in the collection of snippets from here or there, found mostly on websites, or taken from books that just as likely could have drawn their sources from the World Wide Web as well. Though one cannot remove the possibility that writers and researchers who know where to look will indeed find good data when they need it, sometimes even the "good data" can be taken out of context, which, in truth, may have been the case on a few occasions with Dr. Oberth's statements.

The mid 1960s represented a time less polluted by what, today, are nearly *excessive* amounts of data that have come forth in the form of blogs and news sites, following the advent of the Internet. Magazines like *Fate* were once the best resources for information on subjects like UFOs, and hence, it had also lent a welcome respite for Oberth to delve into his interests on the subject free of ridicule. Farrell, an excellent researcher, cites Oberth correctly of course (sparing minor omissions for the sake of brevity). However, if one reads the entire article, it does seem that Oberth, while formulating a hypothetical approach to UFO studies that involves the potential existence of extraterrestrials, nonetheless attempts to do so objectively, rather than making sensational or apparently misleading claims. At the end of the article, he also addresses the fact that his views toward an extraterrestrial hypothesis should not be taken merely at face value, or misinterpreted as advocacy, but instead as reasoned speculation. And finally, Dr. Oberth also makes it clear that he was already used to getting a fair amount of criticism by the time his piece for *Fate Magazine* had gone to print, based on the supposition that he had been operating under false motives for various clandestine reasons; obviously, this perception still holds true to some degree even today. Thus, his actual statements addressing the matter will be included here, with no redactions, so that his words are less likely to be misconstrued:

> It has been implied in German publications that I profess a belief in space ships from other worlds in order to publicize space travel. This is silly. It is like a manufacturer saying: "But my competitor can do it better!"
>
> I wish to correct another misunderstanding. I have never said "I believe in... " What I did say is:

"It is a possibility which cannot be refuted *a priori* and which should be explored further."

I regard it as my obligation to inform the public and then to say what I think is most reasonable as far as I know. Should it turn out that my opinion is not right, this would be just one more error in my life! Man errs as long as he lives, and I believe that the only man who doesn't make a mistake is the one who doesn't have a thought in his whole life.

I do concern myself with UFO research because it is along the line of space travel and because I believe that objective persons should screen the material which is gathered in commendable fervor even by persons who are not always objective. I believe myself capable of the necessary objectivity. [10]

One can never know fully the motivations of another man's heart; however, Oberth's words here do not appear to be aimed at disseminating falsehoods. But to be fair to all parties, there are still points of interest that Farrell and others have made which may still beg further inquiry, and while there does seem to be some evidence where advanced physics projects that had their beginning in Nazi Germany could have been continued elsewhere after the war, it is difficult to assert whether any of these could account for the more exotic instances of flying objects, or for that matter,

Dr. Hermann Oberth advocated the possibility that some UFOs may be extraterrestrial craft. © NASA, date unknown. Source: Wikipedia

the ghost rockets discussed in UFO literature. And finally, if Oberth had known about these, and had been working just to aid in a cover up by discussing extraterrestrial UFOs openly in his piece for *Fate Magazine*, then he was damned good liar.

So where, then, does this leave us in terms of coming to a fuller understanding of the Nazi-UFO connection, especially in relation to spurious reports of missiles and "ghost rockets" seen after the close of the war? One thing is that, while many have asserted that there are ties to secret Nazi technology that could be made, we have very little evidence to back up the idea that such remarkably advanced technologies had been used by Germany at any point throughout the War. Author Mack Maloney has argued against there being a direct Nazi component to the ghost rocket reports, stating that the technologies observed, especially in cases like the Halberstadt "rocket" from 1944, would have been more advanced than any known rocket technologies the Nazis had at that time:

> The Germans *were* working with rocket technology throughout the war; this was evidenced by the V-1 and V-2 vengeance weapons that would make their presence known by mid-1944.
>
> But at no point did the Nazi war machine ever have a rocket that could find an aerial target in the night sky, fly up to it, get on a parallel course with it and make turns to stay with it, as many of these "rockets" were seen to do.

That kind of technology would require at the very least an elaborate guidance system (either internal or ground- or air-based), complex steering mechanisms built into the rocket fins and a massive fuel tank to allow such a "smart" object to stay airborne for long periods of time. Plus, if it had been some kind of German weapon, why didn't these "rockets" fulfill their missions and destroy Allied war planes instead of just riding alongside them? [11]

Another theory Maloney states, which Allied forces had used to explain such cases, had involved secret weapons like the Hs-293, a rocket-like anti-ship guided missile that the allies had knowledge of. However, Maloney questions just how reliable this craft might have been in terms of its field tests, as the Hs-293 relied upon primitive remote-control technology. In truth, there were more than thirty incidents during the war where the Hs-293 guided missiles had caused damage to warships (a complete listing of these can be accessed easily through the English language Wikipedia entry for the Hs-293). In some instances, these attacks resulted in serious damage or sinking of these vessels, as well as the destruction of infrastructure that included buildings and bridges, though only in a minority of cases. [12]

One thing is clear about these early guided missiles, however, and this is the fact that the Hs-293 units had been designed specifically for targeting ships, not planes. "In the military-think of the time," Maloney concludes, "these objects *had* to be explained in some way. So one British intelligence group decided that what allied aircrews were seeing were indeed Hs-293-type devices either launched from an aircraft of dropped by parachute." [13] As to the tremendous speeds, or the maneuverability the craft seemed to exhibit, these more rare cases were categorically explained as being "defects in the rockets themselves," which caused "erratic behavior." [14]

EPICENTER OF THE ENIGMA: SWEDEN IN 1946, AND THE FIRST GOVERNMENT UFO INVESTIGATION GROUP

As some reports we have reviewed here already indicate, the ghost rocket phenomenon continued on after the war, prompting official interest in countries like Norway, Finland, and Sweden, where a majority of the sightings had taken place. Even the United States and Britain, who had gone on to develop and test their own V-2 rockets based on recovered German technology, could not account for the plethora of reports coming out of Scandinavia at the time, which by the summer of 1946, had entailed what literally became hundreds of reports of missile-like objects seen streaking through the skies. Much the same, the fact that the Soviets, who had been actively working to secure what little technology they had recovered and get it back to the Soviet Union, eliminates another theory that the so-called ghost rockets had been emanating from Peenemunde, as addressed earlier in the passage from Clark and Coleman.

Nonetheless, the sheer number of reports coming in had elicited concern, resulting in what researcher Anders Liljegren called "the world's first UFO investigation group," formed in Sweden in 1946 in response to the ghost rocket craze:

> Sweden was, as far as we know, the first country in the world to appoint a special committee—or delegation—to investigate phenomena of a UFO character. This committee included representatives of the Defence Staff, the Air Administration, the Research Institute of National Defence (FDA), the Defence Radio Institute (FRA) and the Naval Administration. The Air Defence department of the Defence Staff collected all the reports from military and civilian sources. The committee's analytical work was co-ordinated mainly by employees of the Air Administration. [15]

The committee formed on July 10, and began to examine instances of unexplained aerial phenomena being reported in the region. Despite the large number of sighting reports gathered by this specially formed Swedish ghost-rocket committee, it was determined by December of 1946 that any ongoing effort to crack the mystery of the Scandinavian phantom missiles would be fruitless:

> Despite the extensive effort which has been carried out with all available means, there is no actual

proof that a test of rocket projectiles has taken place over Sweden. The committee has therefore been forced to decide that the investigation has been unsuccessful and that it was useless to continue the activity in its present form and with the present limited resources. Even if the main part of the report can be referred to as celestial phenomena, the committee cannot dismiss certain facts as being merely public imagination. [16]

Researchers Clas Svahn and Anders Liljegren later interviewed Sweden's Defence Staff secretary at the time, Eric Malmberg, who had been a member of the committee. Malmberg expressed his views on the strange missiles seen in his home country four decades earlier, noting that he and his colleagues did feel a number of the cases had been legitimate. Still, no complete determination could be made, then or now, as to the origin of what had seemingly been, at the time, a non-existent technology:

> I would like to say that everyone on the committee, as well as the chairman himself, was sure that the observed phenomena didn't originate from the Soviet Union. Nothing pointed to that solution. If the observations were correct, many details suggest that it was some kind of a cruise missile. But nobody had that kind of sophisticated technology in 1946. [17]

The Scandinavian countries, which had been home to the majority of the early incidents with missiles and projectiles of unknown origin, actually have an even longer history of documented reports with unidentified avionic wonders. Reports of strange aircraft that predate the Second World War indicate that something was being seen in skies over northwestern Europe much earlier, with specific focus on the winters of 1933-34 and then again in 1936-37. The Swedish Aviation Historical Society, *Svensk Flyghistorisk Förening,* have featured a number of articles on the subject, which have been corroborated with documentation found in the files of the Military Record Office in Stockholm and other groups. [18] These "ghost fliers," as they came to be known, were often described as resembling conventional aircraft, rather than anything exotic or otherworldly. However, they were considered anomalous, like the later reports of ghost rockets, largely due to the fact that there are no official records known to exist that account for who had been operating them, or what operations they may have been used for.

In truth, the majority of the incidents described here might indeed have had conventional explanations, or at least a terrestrial source. The technology exhibited in many of these instances—whether the ghost fliers of the 1930s, or their more flamboyant ghost rocket cousins that emerged after the war—had seemed very much like known terrestrial craft; at very least, they had been similar enough to technologies that were either in production already, or would be produced within a few years. It stands to reason

Captured V-2 technology led to new designs in the U.S. and Britain, but where else had this been the case? © NASA, 1950. Source: Wikipedia

that there may indeed have been a technological presence, and maybe one of an terrestrial variety, that had undertaken secretive tests with newly innovated rocket technology... but who, if not Russia or the Allied countries, could have been behind this, and why did they so greatly favor Scandinavia for this ongoing experimentation?

With this latter point in mind, another intriguing element to the mystery that surfaces is how the operations of these mysterious aircraft—whatever their source or purpose—had seemed to specifically favor the Swedish airspace, rather than that of neighboring areas that included Belgium, Denmark, Finland, the Netherlands, Norway, and the Baltic countries. All of the aforementioned had been neutral during World War II; however, Sweden would be the only of these that would succeed at evading attack throughout the conflict. And Sweden, despite its neutrality, had also maintained economic arrangements with Nazi Germany that involved the supply of iron and other metals, in addition to certain quantities of machined parts. Though some might interpret this ominously (especially when reflecting on Sweden's ability to have remained unmolested despite German aggression elsewhere in the region), historians like Carl-Axel Wangel have argued to the contrary that Sweden had been all but *forced* to abide by such arrangements, lest an otherwise inevitable invasion occur. Also, due to the fact that the war had not lasted any longer than it did, aggression between territories in conflict had ceased before Germany or, for that matter, the British were forced to invade Sweden for strategic reasons. [19]

Sweden is nonetheless to be of interest within the context of any historical analysis of the ghost rockets, largely due to this combination of factors that kept them not only neutral and unmolested, but also an economic asset to the Nazis. And here, we should bear in mind again that Sweden would go on to become the first country whose government would assemble a group to investigate unexplained aerial phenomenon. This alone would seem to indicate that Sweden had served as a sort of epicenter for the rocket sightings occurring at the time. But does it provide evidence for any further involvement Sweden may have had with the mystery, particularly in terms of an unusual projectile technology that was being tested there? If this had been the case, then the Allied forces and Russia, as well as those government officials who had served on the Swedish ghost rocket committee, certainly still appeared to be at a loss for explaining who had been behind the technology that employed these strange projectiles. Again, if the objects had been evidence of any secret Earth technology, the question of who had been behind these ghost rockets presents a troubling conundrum, and perhaps an unsettling one.

To allude to there being an ongoing secretive military project following the war, and one of clandestine origin, would indeed require strides upon the unsteady grounds of speculation. However, to append an "extraterrestrial" theory as an alternative would, in this case, seem almost absurd... nearly as absurd, at least, as citing outdated amniocentesis procedures used by alien beings aboard their UFO aircraft for purposes of pregnancy tests during alleged alien abductions. In other words, there is precedent for some speculation in historical research, at least when the alternative is not just unlikely, but mostly impractical. And yet, time and time again, when evidence of a technology of Earthly origin seems to be lacking, researchers have tended to gravitate toward the otherworldly instead. Sadly, a lack of evidence for one quantity cannot be offered as proof of another, or else none of this "ghost rocket" business would still be a matter of debate more than half a century later.

In truth, very little about the early ghost rocket technologies seemed to betray an extraterrestrial component, though some reports certainly hint at a highly advanced technology that had appeared in our midst which, by conventional accounts, should not have existed at the time. Still, this in itself cannot be held as "proof" of alien visitors who, again, had been employing a technology that seemed barely able to exceed what humans had already been well equipped to do at the time with captured German rocket technologies.

AQUATIC ESCAPISTS: ROCKETS PLUNGING INTO LAKES

There is one final point about these ghost rockets that should be made, which, as we will soon see, has become perhaps one of the most consistent aspects of recurring reports pertaining to projectiles of unknown origin. For whatever reason, these objects, very much like a number of UFO reports documented over the years, appear to have some connection with large bodies of water, particularly in the sense that the anomalous projectiles in such cases are either seen emerging from, or traveling into large lakes and oceans. One of the most prominent Scandinavian cases from the 1940s involved the alleged crash of a ghost rocket into Lake Kolmjarv in northern Sweden on July 19, 1946. Such reports, as well as a host of others that involved these ghost rockets crashing into sizable bodies of water, would prompt zoologist Ivan T. Sanderson, a rather prominent researcher of the unexplained a number of decades ago, to question the aquatic connection:

The record of these things is really very aggravating, because there was absolute proof that they were not meteors or any other such so-called natural phenomena, while half the total population of the country appears to have observed them, and they came from all directions and went in all directions. Further, a very high proportion fell down! But, as both official releases and press reports stated at the time: *"Unfortunately it has been impossible to get hold of any of them because all of them have fallen into lakes."*

Now, one has to acknowledge the fact that there are an awful lot of lakes in Sweden. In fact, according to the Swedish Information Service, no less than 10 percent of its land surface is under fresh water. Yet is it not rather odd that *all* of these "flying boxcars," or "V-1s," or whatever else they were described as being at the time, were said to have fallen into lakes? If this was not so, why did anybody say that it *was* so? The old cliché had it that 40 million Frenchmen could not be wrong. This was proved to be baloney in 1940; but that even two of the 7.5 million Swedes could all be hallucinated, and for several months, seems to me to be stretching credibility too far. The bloody things fell down; but all that did so fell into lakes. Why? [20]

There is much more that could be said here about the ghost rocket reports immediately following the war, especially if our only objective while discussing them were aimed at elaborating on reports that have already been well documented elsewhere. Instead, with respect to researchers who have painstakingly worked in the past to uncover and catalogue the tales of strange projectiles seen throughout Scandinavia and other parts of the world, and primarily during the summer of 1946, at this point we will move forward, and look at the lesser-known instances of very similar phenomenon that have persisted throughout the years, and continue even today.

Within the greater context of UFO studies, the Scandinavian ghost rockets, as well as their fleeting cousins elsewhere around the world, are often viewed as having been a relatively isolated phenomenon, especially in the chronological sense. Had this indeed been the case, it would be simpler to assume that perhaps we really were dealing with some kind of secret operation, and that the sensitive nature of the technology those ghost rocket reports actually represented would still be cause for secrecy even today. More simply, perhaps even a technology that seemed so dangerous—and surreal—immediately after the Second World War would just be less attractive to the modern UFO enthusiast, since now these sorts of projectile technologies have seen widespread use, and thus can be accounted for more easily.

What cannot so be so easily explained, however, is the number of reports that have persisted throughout the years, which involve stories of missile-like aircraft and projectiles of unknown origin that are still seen streaking through our skies. Though less sensational in their modern context, and perhaps also less widely distributed, the reports have nonetheless continued into modern times, and their similarity to the earlier ghost rocket sightings, as well as the persistent absence of any suitable explanation for their random appearance, arouses familiar suspicions of an unsettling reality underlying our more general knowledge of modern aviation.

Indeed, a survey of the available literature shows, as we will soon see, that the stories of anomalous missiles and other craft resembling projectiles are far from gone. In many of these cases, which generally remain unknown to the greater public, the chief witnesses have been experienced pilots of commercial or military aircraft, who went on to file reports discussing the troubling nature of what they felt were potentially dangerous projectiles they observed. Like their ancestors, these projectiles would fit the criteria for being "ghost rockets" in the truest sense, and like those stories immediately following the war, these objects maintain a curious proclivity for coming—and going—without ever leaving a clue to their origin. Some evidence even suggests that these objects have been, at times, a deadly presence in our skies.

Chapter Two

Ghost Rockets in the Atomic Age

"The release of atomic energy has not created a new problem. It has merely made more urgent the necessity of solving an existing one."

Albert Einstein

It was on the morning of Friday June 30, 1950, only hours before President Harry S. Truman would give orders for U.S. armed forces to assist in defending South Korea from invading North Korean armies, that something sensational taking place in the skies over Nevada would begin to draw national attention. Many area residents reported observing an odd, unidentified craft that passed through the sky, flying at an extremely high altitude and remaining visible for several minutes as it cruised along. The object, which would become widely reported once newspapers hit the stands Friday morning, had most closely resembled a rocket or projectile of some kind, evidenced by the thick cloud of smoke it produced as it raced across the desert sky.

The craft, whatever it had actually been, first appeared shortly after nine in the evening, local time, on the night of Saturday, June 24, when it was witnessed by a number of area residents, among them the Commissioner of Nye County, Charles Cavanaugh, and his family. A licensed pilot, Cavanaugh told of how he watched a huge, "reverse E" shaped vapor trail emitting from "a darting object of unfamiliar design." The object appeared to be flying at a very high altitude, which Cavanaugh guessed to be much higher than any conventional aircraft, likely between 50,000 and 75,000 feet. [1] Detailed accounts of this American "ghost rocket" appearance went on to be featured in two Nevada-based publications, the *Goldfield News* and the *Beatty Bulletin*, in which headlines described the object as a "Mystery Flame"; however, further reading would almost

immediately betray the use of more popular terminology of
the day in the report that followed:

> The possibility that two Beatty residents may have
> actually seen a flying disc was being discussed
> excitedly here this week. The witnesses are W. H.
> (Brownie) Brown and Claude Looney.
>
> "We were traveling up into Cherry Creek on a
> fishing trip, about 90 miles east of Warm Springs,
> when we saw a strange light in the sky to the
> north," Brownie related. He described it as "a
> spiral affair, almost like a corkscrew."
>
> It was apparently caused by some object flying
> at a tremendous altitude, the vapor trail of which
> "lit up the whole northern sky." [2]

It is interesting to note the spiral-shaped flight path
attributed to the object, as well as the vapor trail that
witnesses were describing, since many modern reports of
UFOs that have been blamed on missile launches, having
taken place in recent years in locations like Norway and
Australia, often describe similar "swirling" patterns in the
vapor trail these objects produce. As with the famous
Norway spiral of 2009, this was attributed to a missile
spinning erratically out of control due to a failure in its
guidance system.

An entire host of similar headlines about "Mystery
Flames" were appearing elsewhere that week. On Tuesday
June 27, page seven of the Reno Nevada *State Journal* ran a

BLAZING OBJECT SEEN CRUISING OVER NEVADA

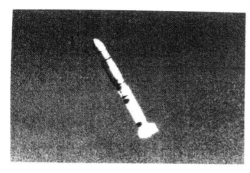

'Saucer' Leaves Vapor Trail as it Rockets Past, Lighting the Evening Sky

NEVADA, A strange spectacle was observed by Nye County residents recently, as a strange object flew high over the desert. Observers agree

What was the object seen over Nevada in the summer of 1950?
© 2013 by Micah Hanks. Missile image source: Wikipedia.

headline that read, "Airline Men See Mystery Flame in Sky." Two days earlier, on June 25, page three of the *Los Angeles Times* carried the similar headline, "Blazing Object Seen Speeding Over Nevada." That same day, the Boise Idaho *Sunday Statesman* detailed an account given by pilots who had also seen this "glowing vapor trail" over Nevada. The *Review-Miner* out of Lovelock, Nevada, would go on to report that a total of *ten* pilots had seen a "Flying Saucer" on Saturday night, and not to be outdone, the *State Journal* followed up in its Sunday edition with an addendum to what the Lovelock pilots had seen, agreeing with the earlier assessment and concluding that, "Maybe It's a Saucer!" [3]

While it didn't actually resemble a saucer in shape, whatever this object was that news agencies had been reporting was apparently seen by hundreds of witnesses, spanning between Nevada, southern California, and the neighboring states of Arizona and Utah. Among the witnesses, a number of experienced commercial airline pilots and their passengers, as well as civilian pilots like Commissioner Cavanaugh, and even some military personnel, had reported the object. Since the craft had been seen just days before the onset of the Korean War, such sightings no doubt may have lent to speculation about secret weapons systems and wartime operations that were already afoot.

Earlier that year, a similar object had been observed as it flew over Tucson, Arizona. In a February 2, 1950 editorial appearing in the *Daily Citizen*, Bob Campbell described the object he had seen as being a projectile of some sort, which even seemed to hover momentarily as it passed over Tucson:

> At what must have been top speed the object spewed out light colored smoke, but almost directly over Tucson it appeared to hover for a few seconds. The smoke puffed out an angry black and then became lighter as the strange missile appeared to gain speed and shoot westward. [4]

Campbell wrote that a radio operator at Davis-Monthan Air Force Base tracked the craft, but wasn't able to identify it. Lieutenant Roy L. Jones Jr., who had been departing from the area at the time in a B-29, was asked to investigate the mystery missile, which, according to Campbell, had veered off toward California and disappeared by that time. "Dr. Edwin F. Carpenter, head of the University of Arizona department of astronomy, said no one at Steward observatory saw the object because none of the staff was viewing the sky at the time," Campbell reported. "However, he was certain of one thing," he continued. "The object was not a meteor or other natural phenomena." [5]

Two years later, a now familiar phenomenon in relation to the reports of anomalous rockets would take place halfway across the world over the Table Bay near Cape Town, South Africa. Ivan Sanderson would document the strange report thusly in his book *Hidden Residents,* which dealt with instances of UFO craft entering, leaving or operating within bodies of water:

> In late 1952 the *Sunday Times* of Cape Town, South Africa, reported that a "rocket" had been seen over Table Bay. It was said to have gone straight up and then down again, but it was not clear if it came out or went into the water. A police launch searched the area since it was believed to have been a distress rocket—but there were no ships in the area. [6]

Curiously, Sanderson goes on to note that, "there are dozens of similar reports of 'distress rockets,' 'flares,' and the like seen off many coasts." Even by as early as the late 1960s when Sanderson had been compiling reports of offbeat semi-aquatic phenomenon for his book, it had apparently been known that anomalous missiles and their appearances continued to be reported, and well after the Scandinavian ghost rockets that surfaced right after the war. However, in our persistent pursuit of the ghost rockets, Sanderson's rather vague statement nonetheless leaves us wishing, as he gives us no idea as to where these "dozens" of reports might be found today.

GHOST ROCKETS OR FLYING SAUCERS?

As to why the sightings of projectiles would not have led to consideration of a more persistent global phenomenon dealing with missiles, rather than saucers, one need not look further than the sorts of news items recounted above. Such cases make clear that the popular term used for virtually *any* kind of anomalous aircraft or other object seen in the skies by the early 1950s, following Kenneth Arnold's sighting of "saucers" in mid 1947, had been "flying saucers" or "flying discs." This was even the case when the reports more accurately described missiles or projectile-like objects. But the great tell-tale, of course, had been that many, if not a majority of these UFOs left vapor trails, just like the objects seen only a few years earlier across the Atlantic. "At that time," Sanderson complained in *Invisible Residents*, with regard to the early rocket reports over Scandinavia, "the stupid moniker 'flying saucer' had not been coined and nobody had thought of the equally stupid designation of 'UFO.' Thus, the stolid, pragmatic Swedes very realistically assumed that these horrible things were some leftovers from the Nazi rocket experimental base of Peenemunde, or that they were devices taken from that place by the Russians and developed during the year or so since the cessation of (World War II) in their country." [7]

Sanderson was not the only person who felt that there might be a legitimate connection between strange aerial phenomenon, likely to be missiles or drones of some sort, and new Russian technology. On January 22, 1953, the *Santa Fe New Mexican* offered the following statement from Dr. Lincoln LaPaz, who would become one of the central figures in the ongoing debate over strange green fireballs that were beginning to appear in the United States with curious frequency:

> A fireball expert said today Russia may be scouting the United States and other parts world with strange new guided missiles. Dr. Lincoln LaPaz said a good many shreds of evidence point to green fireballs sighted throughout the world being a type of missile—possibly of Soviet make. [8]

As later chapters shall reveal, the reports of greenish missiles that fly for great distances while moving parallel to the Earth, rather than merely in descending fashion, would not be a phenomenon that had been specific only to the 1950s. Though often cited in UFO literature, a number of these reports do appear to detail technologies that more closely resemble projectiles—some of them implying intelligent control—that appear capable of moving great distances and at lightning speed. For scientists of the day like LaPaz, it was only natural that a slow and steady lumping together of all the various kinds of UFO craft being witnessed would begin to emerge, and the missile-like aircraft would begin to be referred to as UFOs or, perhaps even worse, merely as "flying saucers."

BOYS OF SUMMER: BOYHOOD ROCKET SIGHTINGS IN THE 1960S AND BEYOND

There are at least a few instances, however, where ghost rockets actually have appeared alongside more typical "saucer" UFOs, even despite the distinctions between legitimate saucer or disc-shaped aircraft, and the anomalous missiles that, by now, had managed to persist under the thin cover of being labeled "saucers." On June 25, 1962, another incident occurred over Tucson that, rather strangely, seemed to involve *both* varieties of objects, where rocket-like projectiles were observed being fired from a large disc-shaped object on the night of June 25, 1962. The witnesses were fourteen-year-old John Westmoreland and his brother James, who were camping along with their neighbor Ronnie Black in a tent in the Westmoreland backyard. The three boys had been playing cards in their tent when, just after nine o'clock in the evening, they described seeing a "flying saucer" (which, in truth, was described as being triangular in shape) hovering in the sky at a fair distance. They observed this craft for a few hours, and at approximately 12:15 AM, it fired "three green things that travelled faster than any plane."

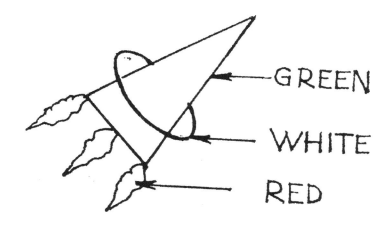

An illustration based on the object witnessed by the Westmoreland brothers. © 1962, Fate Magazine Archives.

Jim and Coral Lorenzen, founders of the Aerial Phenomenon Research Organization (APRO), a now defunct civilian investigational organization that collected and studied UFO reports throughout the 1960s, followed up on the case, detailed in an article Mrs. Lorenzen wrote for the October 1962 issue of *Fate Magazine.* Shortly after the launch of what appeared to be "rockets" from the first craft, the boys then observed what they described as a second flying saucer that appeared in the sky, this time actually bearing a saucer-shape with legs or "stilt-like appendages" protruding from its base. This craft appeared to absorb the "flare-like objects" being launched from the initial craft, then eventually launched what resembled a "rocket" of its own, which sped away at tremendous speed. The sighting concluded shortly afterward, following the appearance of an aircraft the Lorenzens concluded had been a fighter jet from nearby Davis-Monthan Air Force Base, a strategic Air Command installation located within just four miles of the Westmoreland home. [9]

Such incidents involving "rockets" in the United States very likely could have been the result of experimental jet-propelled aircraft in use at the time, rather than actual missiles or warheads of any variety. Modern jet propulsion designs that were employed in America, which would already be in widespread use by the 1950s, had nonetheless been derived largely from captured German wartime technology, stemming from the production of aircraft like the Heinkel He 178 in the late 1930s, which became the first plane to be powered solely using turbojet power. [10] And unlike the Scandinavian rockets, America's jet-propelled "saucers" didn't seem to sport such a penchant for crashing into bodies of water, but instead charged through the sky at what were often impressive altitudes.

A similar incident, having taken place approximately four years after the aforementioned Westmoreland incident, came to light in 2003 after it was logged with the

National UFO Reporting Center (NUFORC), an online resource managed by researcher Peter Davenport that collects and categorizes a number of UFO sightings each year. Like the Westmoreland incident, two brothers, ages five and six, had been standing in the front yard of the farm house where they lived in central Indiana, when they claimed two "rockets" flew directly over them. The objects had moved very quickly, and both men were able to recall the event clearly today, one of them noting in the report filed with the NUFORC that their father had been a pilot, and that they "would have known if it (had been) a couple of jets." It should be noted that the age of the witnesses at the time, however, might cast some doubt on both men's recollection of the incident. [11]

The same summer, a similar incident that involved a low-flying rocket took place over Wayne, Pennsylvania. The witness described seeing a wingless, cigar-shaped object flying at low-altitude "along the 'Main Line' suburbs of Philadelphia." The craft remained visible for approximately half a minute, although despite its altitude, the witness was uncertain in recalling whether the craft produced any sound as it passed overhead:

> To me, the object looked like a rocket, as it was flying low enough that I was sure it had no wings. However, it was not flying vertically... rather, it was flying horizontally, parallel with the ground, as you would watch an airplane or helicopter flying over. Again, there were no wings and no helicopter

blades that I could see. The object was cigar-shaped like a rocket or missile, even though it was flying over land instead of up....

I cannot give an exact date, but it was seen sometime between the middle of June and the middle of August in 1966. This is when I was attending a summer camp at the Valley Forge Military Academy in Wayne, Pennsylvania, about fourteen miles west of Philadelphia. The time of day was, as I recall, late afternoon. [12]

The witness recounts that the sighting had occurred sometime between the middle of June and August of 1966, while attending summer camp at the Valley Forge Military Acadamy in Wayne, Pennsylvania. The craft had appeared sometime in the afternoon:

At that time, I was standing near one of the barracks/dormitories (I believe it may have been Wheeler Hall)... Since the object looked like a rocket or missile, I assumed it was of terrestrial origin. However, I did wonder why a rocket or missile was flying over suburban Philadelphia. [13]

Here again, the witness had been a boy at the time of the sighting, approximately ten years old in this instance, and had neglected to tell anyone about what he had seen on account of the fact that the "vehicle," as he described it, had been moving so quickly that he had no time to notify anyone of its presence. "And," he noted, "Since the vehicle was gone after a few moments, it did not seem to be of much value to tell anyone." [14]

This story seems slightly more credible than the previous rocket incident, involving the witness and his brother who at the time were only five and six, respectively. However, an interesting facet that begins to emerge in relation to alleged reports of rocket-shaped UFOs beginning in the 1960s, and continuing on even throughout the next few decades, is that in many of the cases, the witnesses are young children—typically young boys—and generally between the ages of five and ten (with the exception of the Westmoreland boys, the eldest of whom had been fifteen at the time of their encounter). Another rather telling encounter that seems to fall into this category of boyhood rocket observations allegedly took place on Halloween night, 1976, near the town of Garland, Texas. The witness here described several copper-colored, rocket-shaped objects moving over the street in his neighborhood, and despite the other children and parents who were present at the time (among them had been the witness's mother), no one else seems to have seen the alleged "rockets":

> I was 4 or 5, and it was Halloween. I had been across the street from my house playing with a friend, and my mother came to take me home for bed. I always went to bed around 8:00 (PM). As we were walking across the street, I saw almost directly

over me, and flying over my house (about 10 ft above house), a line of crafts that were copper, and shaped like missiles. They were going pretty slowly, and there were no windows or anything like that. It made no noise. [15]

The witness here, based on his recollection of the childhood event, said he felt there had been "somebody up there watching," and remembered other children in costumes who were out in the street at the time of the observation. At this point, he gestured to the objects, and asked his mother what they were, to which she apparently replied that she couldn't see anything. "I wasn't thinking about aliens," the witness said, instead describing a sensation that he had seen something that no one else around him appeared to be able to observe like he had. Years later, at the time this report was filed with the National UFO Reporting Center, the witness felt it had been very odd, and had begun to question whether there might have been an extraterrestrial component to what he had seen. [16]

Returning to Europe, we find another boyhood rocket encounter that transpired in 1983, at Balderton Newark on Trent, near Nottinghamshire, England. The witness, age ten, had been playing with his elder brother, age fifteen, and the area vicar's son, when they began heading on an easterly course up the street toward the witness's home. At some point, the three children noticed a strange silence that came over the neighborhood, during which all the summer sounds of birdsong, traffic nearby, etc, had seemed to cease altogether. It was during this strange silence that the group of boys claimed to see three missile-shaped objects flying at low altitude over their neighborhood. The primary witness said these objects had been traveling close to roof level with his family's home, moving at approximately 10 miles per hour. The objects were "about two buses in length and about a double bus height," and appeared to have been made of some dark colored metal. Each of the objects had the basic shape of a missile, which included three large fins, and each craft moved noiselessly through the air. The witness also described that these objects produced no flame or exhaust, and that one of the three "missiles" had appeared to travel not above or around, but *through* his parent's house, "like a magician walking through a wall." [17]

In truth, these samples depict only a small portion of a much greater cross-section of reports in UFO literature, which seem to relate otherworldly encounters experienced by young boys in their elementary or preteen years. While their consistency to one another does not necessarily rule them out as being hoaxes or confabulation, it is interesting to note that there are often fantastic elements related in such cases, the likes of a presumably large missile-like object passing directly through brick and mortar in almost spectral fashion, or strange, exotic-looking "missiles" that had been seen by only one child, who became the sole witness to an encounter with copper-colored ghost rockets even after pointing the craft out to his mother. Do such reports highlight the curious propensity for the child's mind to fabricate, confuse, or simply orchestrate a reality all to themselves, and especially during the first decade of their young lives? Also, the fact that each of these cases, going all the way back to the Westmoreland brothers in the early 1960s, has to do with young boys may be a key to fully understanding such reports; had the witnesses been girls instead, would they have been as prone to describe seeing large projectiles or other potentially deadly and destructive objects? Again, this is not to say that many of these young male witnesses over the years hadn't seen anything at all. However, the realistic potential for the creation of false memories on account of an overly impressionable young mind (particularly with those reports where witnesses were between five and ten years of age) must be given fair consideration, especially when such striking similarities continue to emerge decade after decade.

By the late 1960s and throughout the 1970s, reports of objects that unambiguously fit the descriptions of rockets or missiles would begin dying off somewhat, despite what could be viewed historically as an almost inverse increase in reports of saucers and other kinds of unidentified aircraft. The mid-to-late 1960s also would come to represent a period during which UFO craft being witnessed near missile silos, projectile test ranges, and nuclear sites would become a consistent enigma; whatever these strange craft may have been, they appeared to be capable of influencing the launch systems at such locations, with a number of reported incidents emerging over the years which detail system shutdowns and missile launch failures, especially while unidentified objects were seen nearby.

Despite the apparent die-off in ghost-rocket reports during this period, a handful of projectile incidents have nonetheless been documented (see Appendix A for a complete chronological listing of ghost rocket sightings, which includes a number of reports from the 60s and 70s). However, with the increase in reports of various other kinds of craft during this period—some of them resembling projectiles of massive size—it is important to advise that caution be used in classifying such aircraft as genuine "projectiles," since many of these craft, in addition to being far bigger than any known guided missiles or rockets in use at the time, had also likely been manned aircraft of some variety. Clues to the origins of such mysterious craft, on the other hand, still remain sparse, and thus speculation regarding extraordinary vehicles of "alien" origin has been proposed over the years, in an effort to account for such bizarre and seemingly impossible vehicles.

THE CURIOUS CASE OF THE FLYING CIGARS

Whatever their origins may have been, it seems undeniable that a variety of aircraft that was entirely different from anything known to man at the time had begun to appear by around the late 1940s. In particular, these craft were much larger than manmade projectiles—sometimes estimated to be 100 feet in length or more—and while not true "ghost rockets," these craft bear enough similarity to rockets in their apparent function that their mention here, albeit briefly, warrants some historical consideration. If anything, the presence of a technology that seemed to be using highly advanced rocket propulsion in such exotic ways—whether for the drone-like ghost rockets, or for a much larger, manned craft of some variety—suggests there may indeed have been a broader-reaching operation underlying these mysterious and exotic looking projectile technologies.

At the outset of the 1940s-era ghost rocket reports detailed in this essay, we took a moment to examine the case of Captain Jack Puckett, who in 1946 observed a strange rocket-like object with a "cylindrical shape approximately twice the size of a B-29 bomber, with luminous portholes." The craft had no wings, though it did produce a sparkling exhaust trail of sorts as it careened past Puckett and his crew at tremendous speed; certainly, the description of this craft, aside from being *huge* by the aviation standards of the day, sounded very much like something akin to advanced rocket propulsion.

Had this been a one-off, we might have filed Puckett's sighting alongside the other bizarre reports of phenomenon that, while vaguely resembling Earth technologies, would better fit the colorful pages of a sci-fi comic book. After all, what kind of an aircraft would be capable of flight under such extremities: a tremendous fuselage, bigger than a B-29, but without wings, and capable of traveling at dangerously fast speeds, all the while propelled through the air by what could only have been a nuclear thruster that bore no

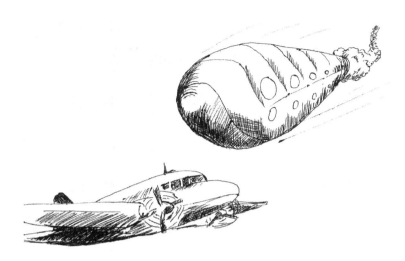

The Chiles and Whitted Encounter. © 2013, art by Micah Hanks.

promise of ever safely returning its crew back to its home base? It seems too outlandish to even be taken seriously.

But the reports of this aircraft, strange as they were, would continue, specifically involving some odd, elongated craft that had two rows of windows along its long, straight and wingless fuselage. In fact, what could easily have been the same craft Puckett observed in 1946 was later seen over Alabama on July 24, 1948, nearly colliding with an Eastern Airlines DC-3. Pilot Clarence Chiles and co-pilot John Whitted observed the strange torpedo-shaped object in the early morning at an altitude of approximately 5000 feet. Both agreed that it was approximately 100 feet long, nearly three times the diameter of a B-29 bomber, and produced a reddish exhaust trail. The craft had two rows of windows along its side, suggesting an upper and lower deck, which appeared to be brightly illuminated from within.

These encounters, as well as the one that follows, have been well documented already, and if anything, more times than is probably necessary. However, a later encounter with a long, cigar shaped object similar to the ones encountered in 1946 and 1948 would go on to become one of the best known UFO encounters of the 1970s, involving four men aboard an Army Reserve UH-1 Huey helicopter near Mansfield, Ohio, on October 18, 1973.

The crew, consisting of Captain Lawrence Coyne, along with Lieutenant Arrigo Jezzi, Seargent John Healy, and Spec. 5 Robert Yanacsek, had been retuning from a regularly scheduled medical examination. Just before 11 PM that evening, one of the men noticed a bright red light off in the distance to the south, followed by the appearance of a red light to the east. The object began to move toward the helicopter, and soon the crew aboard the Huey had begun a sharp descent in order to try and evade a collision with the object. As they plummeted through the air, Coyne and his crew reached a descending speed of close to 2000 miles per hour, and noticed they had lost radio contact with the operators at Mansfield Approach Control. By the time the helicopter stabilized, the approaching aircraft was directly over them, which appeared to be a long, blimp-like body fitted with a large red light, as well as a bright green light which acted similar to a spotlight that was directed toward them. After approximately ten seconds, the craft began to move away, and gradually accelerated as it left the scene, flying toward the northwest. [18]

As to what sort of craft Coyne and his crew encountered in 1973 is anyone's guess. However, it seems clear that a number of cases involving objects described as projectiles could be reports of similar craft, especially when seen from a distance. It becomes difficult at times to understand precisely what is going on, with all the varieties of different aircraft reported throughout different avenues of UFO research and literature. The aforementioned Chiles and Whitted encounter had apparently led early Air Force UFO investigations under what was then known as Project Sign to look into the possibility of a "wingless fuselage" the likes of what these pilots claimed to witness, and discern whether it were actually a design that could be capable of flight. Some of the Project Sign researchers, including Captain Robert Sneider, thought such a craft could potentially fly, especially given the promises of the nuclear era, which he detailed in his official report on the incident. [19] Could there indeed have been some variety of advanced, and incredibly powerful technology that was not only propelling the ghost rockets through the air, but also had been employed for some varieties of aircraft that actually contained passengers? If so, who, or *what*, might these passengers have been?

During the middle to late 1970s, even the reports of cigar shaped objects would begin to diminish somewhat, along with a marked decrease in reports of missile-like objects. In truth, there are a number of possible reasons for this apparent decline in projectile sightings: for one, the reports of more exotic-sounding aircraft, especially the enigmatic saucers and craft that were often both brilliantly and colorfully lit, were by far the more sensational of the UFO incidents being recorded at the time. In addition to the reports of physical UFOs that were witnessed, there had also been an entirely new facet of the ongoing UFO enigma that would begin to emerge during this period: abductions of human beings by the presumed occupants of these strange craft. Unlike the more dubious "contactee" claims of the previous decades, abduction reports seemed to be less likely the result of willful misrepresentation of hucksters and charlatans, and instead represented a handful of incidents where individuals appeared to be genuinely alarmed by an invasion into their lives that both frightened and amazed them. Cases like the famous 1973 "Pascagoula Incident," which involved the alleged abduction of two shipyard employees named Charles Hickson and Calvin Parker, would begin to represent a relatively new aspect of the ongoing UFO phenomenon that was both unsettling, and largely inexplicable.

In addition to the overshadowing rendered by such high-profile UFO cases, there was also a well-defined effort toward dismissal that had been brought before the public by October of 1968. Conveniently planned for Halloween of that year, the Colorado UFO Project delivered its final report, which both failed to find anything significant to UFO studies, and also led to the closure of the Air Force Project Blue Book, which at the time had presented the most enduring study of UFO phenomenon by an official body since its institution in the early 1950s. Following the so-called "Condon Committee", the UFO subject would begin to see a noticeable decrease in serious treatment by the mainstream press, and thus, reports of rockets or projectiles that might have seemed too extraordinary could very likely have been dismissed purely as more dispatches from the lunatic fringe, which UFO advocates had already become known to represent before academia and the serious news agencies.

Thus, whether or not many of these American reports emanating from the sixties and seventies can be taken as reliable cases involving rockets cruising through American airspace, elsewhere around the world the troubling presence of phantom missiles would not only continue, but would begin to pose a potentially grave and destructive threat. This would be made shockingly evident in a handful of deadly incidents that, to this day, remain largely unreported in UFO circles; perhaps this is understandable, since in many of these cases, although the mystery objects might be ufological in nature by conventional standards, they nonetheless seem to point to something more complex and, at times, perhaps even sinister that had been taking place in a few isolated incidents around the globe. Whether they had been accidents, or the result of planned events, the devastating nature of the reports that follow would set a new precedent for incidents that involved anomalous projectiles spanning the next several decades.

THE AER LINGUS FLIGHT 712 INCIDENT

The same year that Edward Condon and his associates had given their public statement on the merit of UFO research, March 24, 1968 would also mark one of the most devastating passenger plane accidents of the decade: the crash of Irish Aer Lingus Flight 712.

Flight 712 had been a Vickers Viscount 803, nicknamed "Saint Phelim," which was flying from Cork to London when it crashed inexplicably into the sea off the southeast coast of Tuskar Rock, in County Wexford. The craft had departed from Cork at approximately 10:32 AM local time, and by 10:57 AM had reached the Bannow reporting point. Here, they were advised to change their frequency for communication with London Air Traffic Control, which was completed, and contact was made. However, less than ten seconds after establishing contact with London ATC, Flight 712 would deliver a cryptic sounding message, and though it had been difficult to make out, ATC operators discerned that the pilots on board were indicating that Flight 712 was in some kind of danger, saying they were, "Twelve thousand feet descending spinning rapidly". The resulting crash claimed the lives of all 61 people on board. [20]

The initial report on the cause of the accident was published in 1970, conducted by officials with the Aeronautical Section of the Department of Transport and Power, who were unable to determine an exact cause for the crash, and as for any probable cause, the report stated as much, though suggesting some strange "impairment of aircraft controllability" had contributed:

> There is not enough evidence available on which to reach a conclusion of reasonable probability as to the initial cause of this accident. The probable cause of the final impact with the sea was impairment of the controllability of the aircraft in the fore and aft (pitching) plane. [21]

Around the time of the crash, however, speculation had been high that the mysterious crash had involved some other airborne object, possibly an experimental aircraft, military drone, or even a missile. Three decades would pass before officials in Ireland and Britain decided to reopen the case, based on the notion that "the possibility of a cause other than a (near) collision with another airborne object being the initial cause of the upset... does not appear to have been adequately examined in the 1970 Report." However, subsequent examination of the evidence would lead to an independently commissioned study by the Irish Minister for Public Enterprise in 1999, which maintained that there had been no secondary object that crashed into Flight 712. However, there were a number of discrepancies in the data that existed pertaining to transmissions by the crew aboard Flight 172 and nearly 50 witnesses that had been interviewed, as well as the insinuation that paperwork regarding inspection of the aircraft had gone missing, possibly as a sort of internal cover for ineptitude in recognizing flight safety issues. Thus, the final cause of the crash, according to the new report, was stated as follows:

> The initial upset occurred circa 10.40 hours GMT at about FL90 during the climb above the village of Old Parish in County Waterford. The aircraft was recovered from the dive and flew an erratic path inland until 10.58 GMT when there was a second spin or spiral dive from which the crew also recovered the aircraft. Total loss of control then occurred some minutes later near Tuskar Rock. [22]

Despite the missing inspection files dating back to the time of the original investigation, the Saint Phelim aircraft had nonetheless undergone what was described as a "major inspection three weeks earlier." [23] Additionally, there had been questions raised with regard to numerous rather odd delays that held up a more timely recovery of the aircraft following the crash:

> It took 70 days to find the wreckage, despite several reports which pinpointed where it was finally discovered. A local trawlerman, Billy Bates, found it on his first visit there. He says the navy had told him it had looked there three times already.
>
> The search team on HMS Reclaim then tried to raise the fuselage without using a steel net. It scattered as it broke the surface and sunk to the

seabed. With it went many of the victims, and any chance of discovering what had happened. [24]

In addition to the strange delays that had occurred in recovering the Saint Phelim, it was also known that missile tests were being conducted rather frequently in the area at that time, specifically around a testing range near Aberporth, which involved the use of decommissioned RAF Meteor jets for "target practice." These jet aircraft had been among the first in use by the British government, beginning in the waning years of the Second World War. Controversy erupted again in 1974, just six years after the Saint Phelim and her crew met their tragic fate, when the remains of one of these jets had been discovered near Tuskar Rock, where the Saint Phelim had crashed. The RAF insisted that the wreckage had somehow floated to this location, and that testing would have taken place elsewhere. However, area fishermen, who were already skeptical of the incident following the delays in recovery of Flight 712, argued that, "currents and tides make that impossible." [25] Swedish researchers Clas Svahn and Anders Liljegren also reported in early 1993 that "parts of an RPV-like missile were fished out of the sea" the same year, although it is unclear as to whether this information was actually referring to the recovery of the aforementioned Meteor jet components at Tuskar Rock. [26]

Remarkably, there was evidence of yet another unmanned aircraft that some believed might have been responsible for the crash. Portions of a radio controlled target drone known as a SD2 Stiletto had also been recovered from within the vicinity of the crash area, which the British Ministry of Defense had stated could not be associated with missile tests in the area, since no launch system for the craft existed at the time. However, in 2000 Bernard Moffatt wrote in a Celtic League press document that there had been questions regarding the accuracy of this statement:

> The League has queried the accuracy of some of the evidence supplied by the UK for that review. The British MOD had said that parts of a SD2 Stiletto target drone found near the crash site could not be connected with the crash as in 1968 no launch system had been developed for the type. However, we have pointed out that Shorts the Belfast plane maker modified an obsolete Canberra bomber as a launch vehicle for the type in 1967. [27]

The final point of interest involving a projectile theory for the accident involved discrepancies in the log books kept regarding missile launches; while the British Ministry of Defense claimed that the range would have been closed on the day the crash occurred, having been a Sunday, researchers with the Irish news broadcasting agency RTE found that inconsistencies in those records suggested that tests could indeed have taken place the day of the crash. [28]

However, the results of the official 1999 study, as well as subsequent reviews and investigations that continued through the 2000s, specifically a 2002 study by French and Australian experts with the Air Accident Investigation Unit, concluded that the most likely cause for the crash had nonetheless been "a result of structural failure of the aircraft, corrosion, metal fatigue, "flutter" or bird strike." [29]

Much like the prevalence of reports where anomalous missiles and ghost rockets appeared close to large bodies of water, belief in missile strikes to account for otherwise unexplainable passenger plane crashes would again prove to be an engaging theory over the years. This was particularly the case involving one famous and widely reported incident that would occur within two decades of the Aer Lingus incident in 1968, which will be examined here in greater detail at a later time. However, the interim years leading up to that period, specifically throughout the 1980s, would continue to provide a number of haunting reports of strange and unidentified missiles that continued to be observed by passengers, pilots, and a host of others. If a survey of the next few decades could provide any accurate indication of their presence, it would seem that the famous and enigmatic ghost rockets, born out of those paranoia-ridden years just after World War II, were indeed still alive and well. If anything, it would seem that they were soon destined to become a new and frightening global phenomenon.

Chapter Three

The Mystery Missiles: Cold War and Cover Ups

"The [Ustica Massacre] occurred following a military interception... the DC9 was shot down, the lives of 81 innocent citizens were destroyed by an action properly described as an act of war, real war undeclared, [and] a covert international police action against our country, which violated its borders and rights."

Italian Senator Giovanni Pellegrino, 1989.

The expression "Ten Minutes of Mayhem" might only begin to convey the kind of panic radar operators in the United States felt on at least two occasions decades ago, occurring within just months of each other, where it was believed that nuclear missiles were bound for America from the USSR. On the morning of November 9, 1979, what would later prove to be a false alarm erupted into sheer panic for close to ten minutes, after a training tape had given the convincing impression that America was under attack. Then the following June, a computer chip malfunction caused a similar incident, where random numbers of tracks appeared on radar that were initially interpreted to be missiles en route from Russia. [1]

History shows that the Soviets had their own momentary brushes with Armageddon, just as well. In what became known as the Soviet "Autumn Equinox" incident, Soviet early warning satellites interpreted a peculiar alignment of atmospheric conditions as a potential launch from U.S. missile fields. This false alarm might have led to war, if not for Lt. Col. Stanislav Petrov, who after observing the anomalous configuration from the Soviet Serpukhov-15 bunker, chose not to alert his superiors. "When people start a war," he famously said, "they don't start it with only five missiles. You can do little damage with just five missiles." [2]

The same might not be said of just one missile, however, and this became evident on the morning of January 25, 1995, when a joint project between Norwegian and American scientists launched a large sounding rocket from Andoya Island, Norway. Unlike many of that era, this rocket had only been aimed at studying the famous northern lights; however, viewed from Russia, this projectile was following a path similar to that which they felt the U.S. might use to blind Russian radar systems. Fortunately, it soon became evident that Soviet radar defense systems were all still operative, and what became known as the Norwegian Rocket Incident went from being a high alert situation, to a final, but narrow miss with catastrophe. [3]

Throughout the Cold War, incidents such as these remained secret for obvious reasons, though after the fall of the Iron Curtain, such cases were expressed more openly both for historical and precautionary reasons. However, less widely or openly discussed, even after the Cold War years, were the reports of isolated, anomalous missile-related incidents that had proliferated throughout the world at the time, many of which remain unexplained even today.

THE USTICA MASSACRE

In what became the most tragic and deadly incident to ever involve a McDonnell Douglas DC-9-15 in flight, Aerolinee Itavia Flight 870 was performing a routine flight bound for Palermo, Sicili, after departing from Guglielmo Marconi Airport two hours behind schedule on the evening of June 27, 1980. The plane had previously been in contact with ATC in Rome, when approximately one hour after takeoff, Flight 870 would vanish from radar screens, immediately following "an exclamation of surprise" issued by the pilot just as he had begun his ground descent.

Two Italian fighter jets begin the search for the missing Flight 870. ©
U.S. Air Force, 1987. Source: Wikipedia.

The Italian Air Force immediately scrambled a pair of F-104s to try and locate the missing DC-9, but leaving shortly after nine in the evening from Grosseto Air Force Base, it was nearly impossible for them to spot any of the presumed wreckage or survivors that night. Nonetheless, the plane was found within a few hours, having crashed into the Tyrhennian Sea near the island of Ustica. There were no survivors among the 77 passengers on board, nor the two pilots or pair of flight attendants accompanying them. To this day, the Italian government has issued no official explanation as to the cause of this strange and troubling incident. [3]

The Ustica Massacre, as it came to be known, was eventually portrayed as the subject of a film, a number of books, and even a museum display. Despite there being no official stated cause of the DC-9's crash that evening, Italian authorities seemed adamant about the fact that this had been, if not a terrorist act, an undeclared act of outright war. "Radar evidence showed that there had been intense military activity in the area on the night Flight 870 was heading innocently towards Palermo," the *Guardian* reported in 2006, "including the presence of US, French and Libyan military aircraft and an aircraft carrier that, according to some reports, was British." One of the conspiracy theories regarding the incident had been that none other than Muammar Gaddafi, the now deceased former Prime Minister of Libya, had been aboard a transport plane that was the target of an international assassination plot. According to Judge Rosario Priore, an Italian expert on terrorism cases and a respected legal figure in the country, "the passenger jet had either been brought down by a missile or had plunged into the sea after swerving to avoid a mid-air collision with one of the jetfighters." Priore further stated that his previous attempts at getting to the bottom of the disaster, "had been deliberately obstructed by the Italian military and members of the secret service, who had complied with requests from NATO to

cover up the tragedy." [4] Even the former Italian President
Francesco Cossiga had gone on the record expressing the
belief that there had likely been a missile involved with the
crash. [5] However, despite various theories regarding where,
precisely, this missile could have originated, no hard
evidence supporting any of them have been forthcoming.
One thing, however, is certain: recovered wreckage of Flight
870 had seemed to indicate a missile attack:

> Aviation Week and Space Technology bolstered
> the report by publishing that the damage to the
> airliner's fuselage was consistent with... a contin-
> uous-rod missile warhead as employed in air-to-air
> missiles. Any doubts of military involvement in the
> events were rapidly fading—but whose military?
> Were the Libyans responsible for an act of air-to-
> air terrorism? Was it someone else? [6]

GHOST ROCKETS OVER THE BAHAMAS?

Another rocket incident, though a far less destructive
one, occurred at sea in the mid 1980s, as reported by one
of the two witnesses to the National UFO Reporting Center
in 2007. The primary observer had been working with the
RCA Service Company at the Atlantic Underwater Test and
Evaluation Center (AUTEC) base in the Bahamas, at a
location called Andros Island, which forms the western
border of a deep oceanic trench in the Bahamas called the
Tongue of the Ocean (TOTO).

The witness had been a crewmember there in 1985, specializing in work on a variety of torpedo retrieval boats and other sonar testing vessels. On one occasion, he had joined a crew headed for West Palm Beach, Florida, on

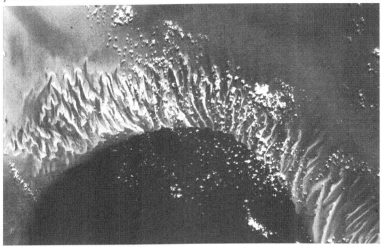

The Tongue of the Ocean, as seen from the Space Shuttle in February 2000. © NASA/JPL/UCSD/JSC 2000. Source: Jet Propulsion Laboratory.

one of the AUTEC vessels, which at the time had been sailing toward the north end of Andros Island, only a short distance from nearby Providence Island, which forms the Eastern border of the TOTO. He and another crewmember were performing a routine overnight watch that lasted from midnight until 4 AM the following morning, when they observed two strange "rockets" flying side by side, which passed directly over their ship traveling on an easterly course:

These "rockets" were highly unusual as neither made any sound, were traveling at an oddly slow rate of speed and were visible to us for about 15 seconds. However, the rockets left behind contrails that glowed brightly and which were "multi-colored," in that the contrail smoke changed from white to green to blue to pink and then disappeared completely after about ten minutes. (I estimate that they passed over us at an altitude of about 500 to 1000 feet; both rockets were white-colored and perhaps 25 to 40 feet in length). [7]

Both the witnesses were baffled by these strange illuminations, and wondered whether the strange projectiles could have been part of some secret U.S. Navy test that had been underway in the area. However, the witness felt that any AUTEC personnel would have possessed knowledge of U.S. Navy experiments in the area, which had certainly not been the case in this instance. "As an AUTEC vessel, we would definitely have been informed that such a test was being undertaken," the witness stated, "and subsequently warned to stay out of the area. This had always been the Navy's practice during similar rocket firing tests that I witnessed while working at sea in the same area." [8] Whatever these two strange objects were, they had been of a mysterious nature, and of unknown origin.

The witness then decided to follow up with an air traffic control operator back at the Andros base, who said he had no knowledge of rocket tests that had taken place on the night the sighting had occurred, though he "certainly would have been in a position to know." [9]

A number of peculiar details stand out with regard to this strange incident. For one, the witness claimed that there had been no knowledge of an experiment taking place that night anywhere nearby, nor did any of the officials or crewmembers he spoke with seem to even so much as hint at knowledge of such an operation. Also, the fact that the two rockets had been flying at a relatively low observational altitude, passing directly over the AUTEC vessel, is curious. But the actual physical proximity between the two rockets had been perhaps the most curious element of all. The witness stated that he had, "never heard of rockets that travel in such close proximity to each other," or "at such an unusually slow speed."

"Since that incident occurred," the witness concluded, "I have learned that there is a known history of so-called ghost rocket sightings in other parts of the world, particularly in Sweden." [10] Could these two objects witnessed by two AUTEC crewmembers in the summer of 1985 have been anything akin to the mysterious projectiles observed over Scandinavia almost half a century earlier?

THE 1985 GHOST ROCKET FLAP CONTINUES

On Monday August 12, 1985, a Japanese Airlines domestic flight en route to Osaka International Airport began to experience problems associated with a series of mechanical failures that occurred only minutes after takeoff.

Approximately one half hour later, JAL 123 would crash into Mount Takamagahara, some sixty-two miles from Tokyo, and despite there being four survivors of the crash, it remains the deadliest single-aircraft accident in aviation history. [11]

The Japanese Airlines 123 incident, while tragic, had not involved any sort of mysterious projectiles. However, just three days later, Greek Olympic Airways Flight 132 had been carrying 61 passengers to Athens when the pilot observed a strange object as they passed over the Swiss-Italian border. Captain Christos Stamulis contacted air traffic control at Linate, Italy, and described to operators that he had just witnessed "a projectile without wings" pass Flight 132 on a horizontal path. The object Stamulis saw had been dark colored, and approximately two meters in length. While Stamulis felt the plane had only barely avoided a collision with the object, none of the passengers on board reported witnessing this strange projectile.

It was confirmed that a Swiss military operation had ended within minutes of the dark projectile's appearance near Saint Gottard, during which civilian air traffic had been restricted for safety reasons. This operation hadn't involved any missiles, however. Researchers Svahn and Liljegren, arguably two of the most prolific chroniclers of the ongoing ghost rocket enigma, noted that there had been rocket systems in use by the Swiss, but to assume that these had been the culprit in the Flight 132 case would also present a number of inconsistencies:

The Swiss military had three rocket systems at the time: Bloodhound, Rapier and Sidewinder. None had been actively used from Swiss territory. The Swiss Sidewinders have only been tested at the north-Swedish missile test area near Vidsel (sometimes used by the military forces of other neutral countries). [12]

Furthermore, Svahn and Liljegren felt that the object had more likely come from the direction of Italy, although Italian authorities flatly refuted this determination:

Judging from its direction of flight, the projectile must have come from the Italian side of the border. Italian authorities denied knowledge of any military tests. The missile had, reportedly, not shown up on military radar and neither Italy nor NATO had anything going on that could explain the sighting. [13]

Other theories (which would bear remarkable similarities to modern reports, such as the Glasgow Airport incident cited in this essay's introduction) included the possibility that a balloon, rather than a missile, could have accounted for the object Captain Samulis witnessed. He disagreed, however, stating that what he had seen, "was a military device, of that I am sure. It was a ballistic rocket." [14]

Remarkably, another missile incident would occur within just three days of the Flight 132 sighting, this time bringing the ghost rocket phenomenon back home to Sweden. The incident involved a Cessna being flown by Per Lundqvist, who was joined by three friends—all of them pilots—on board. The four friends were flying south along the eastern coast of Sweden when they noticed a strange object reflecting sunlight, moving over a forested area:

> [W]e saw that it was a metallic missile with steering fins at the back. Now and then it changed its course according to the terrain and I interpreted this as if it was following the power lines below us... Since we had become curious I dived down towards the missile and turned our plane to try to follow, but this was impossible. We simply didn't have the engine power to compete with the object. It disappeared from us at an altitude of a few hundred meters. [15]

This incident, in typical fashion, was reported to Swedish military authorities, though no direct contact would be made with the pilots from authorities after filing their report. The object report was investigated for another few months, and then dropped again, which begs the question of whether ineptitude, or sheer lack of interest, had been the motivating factor in their treatment of the report.

The missile craze of 1985 would spill over into the years that followed, with reports of strange projectiles coming in from all parts of the world, including parts of Europe, Australia, and eventually again in the United States. On

June 25, 1987, while elsewhere a conference was underway at the National Press Club regarding the so-called "Project Aquarius" and investigation of UFO-related incidents at Kirtland AFB, yet another commercial aircraft was about to have a near-miss with an unidentified flying missile.

Delta Airlines Flight 1083, a Boeing 737 carrying 63 passengers en route to Atlanta, was passing over West Virginia when Captain William Cantrell spotted a missile, headed directly for the 737, at an altitude of approximately 29,500 feet. The object quickly veered off course, missing Flight 1083 by what may have been only a few yards. Researcher Stan Gordon managed to obtain an FAA report on the incident, in which Captain Cantrell had given this description of the object:

> [T]he missile had a short 4" squatty "Homemade" appearance. He described the projectile as approximately 4-6 feet long with large fins attached which ran halfway up its length. The main body of the missile was a white and yellow color and the fins were a beige to brown color. He said it appeared to be descending and unpowered when it passed below him. The pilot stated that he took no evasive action. [15]

Again, the general theories proposed with regard to missile sightings like that which Cantrell and others had observed typically involved balloons or other "hobbyist" activities; this solution seemed especially comfortable for officials to use when the projectiles did not appear to be accompanied by anything similar to smoke or exhaust trails. Around the same time as the Flight 1083 incident, the U.S. Air Force had been recently experimenting with the launch of a new series of MX missiles, fired from a modified Minuteman 3 silo located at Vandenberg Air Force Base in the spring of 1987. Dubbed the "Peacekeeper" by then President Ronald Reagan, these test flights involved the launch of 20 such intercontinental ballistic missiles; however, these launches did not seem to coincide with the appearance of a "missile" observed over West Virginia in June of that year, nor did the trajectories seem to match; the

The "Peacekeeper" ICBM: did test launches of this projectile lead to "ghost rocket" sightings during the 1980s? © DOD Defense Visual Information Center. Source: Wikipedia.

Peacekeepers had been fired toward a target 4,100 miles away in the Pacific Ocean. [16]

So what were the strange rockets seen throughout the 1980s, and was there any explanation for their presence? A review of the reports makes it appear less likely that they can all be attributed to a single underlying cause; some would appear to point to NATO operations, as with the case of the Italian Ustica Massacre and the Greek "ballistic rocket" seen by Captain Stamulis, whereas some of the incidents, like the Swedish reappearance of a "ghost rocket" in 1985, appears to deal with a far more curious underlying phenomenon. Whether or not the ghost rockets could be attributed to a singular clandestine source, it is strange not only that these objects would continue to appear, but that their physical traits would so closely resemble that of various known airborne implements of destruction.

The continuation of rocket reports would not be relegated to the 1980s, however. During the months leading up to the official dissolution of the USSR in December of 1991 and, thus, the end of the Cold War, a number of reports would continue to emanate mostly from over British airspace. An incident was reported by an Italian airliner en route to London on April 21, 1991, involving something "like a missile" seen over the English Channel; barely a month later, a pilot with Britannia Airways would report the first of two encounters the charter airline would have that year, described as "a yellow-orange cylindrical body" bearing a "wrinkled appearance". The following month in July, a second Britannia Airways flight would observe a "small black lozenge shaped object" passing above them, narrowly missing a collision. That same summer, passengers aboard Dan Air Flight DA 4700—also flying out of London—witnessed a grey cigar-shaped object which left no vapor trail, that passed below the plane. [17]

While these reports of missile-like objects are compelling, in some of the instances, such as the first of the two Britannia Airways encounters, a balloon might indeed fit the description of the elongated, but curiously "wrinkled" object. Also, passengers who observed the UFO from aboard Dan Air Flight 4700 were uncertain as to whether the projectile-shaped object, which produced no exhaust, had been flying, or merely hovering once it appeared above the cloud deck below. If the object had managed to keep a fixed position in the sky, then it wouldn't likely have fit the definition of a conventional missile of any kind; but this also

Illustration of the hypersonic-speed X-51 WaveRider scramjet. © U.S. Air Force, 2009. Source: Wikipedia.

leaves questions as to what else the object could possibly have been.

Experimental government craft might still also account for a number of ghost rocket sightings, as well. In an incident eerily reminiscent of the strange aerial "cigars" mentioned previously, on August 5, 1992 the crew of United Airlines Flight 934 observed an unidentified object flying near them (which, strangely, had apparently also been a London-bound flight around the same time). The craft was said to resemble a Lockheed SR-71 without wings, bearing rounded edges, and flying at supersonic speed. [18] The object described here sounds very much like the Boeing Company's X-51 WaveRider "scramjet," an un- manned aircraft capable of attaining speeds exceeding Mach 5 (more than 3000 miles per hour) and travelling 260 miles in just six minutes. While the X-51 has now been retired, it is estimated that the Pentagon had put an estimated $2 billion into research for similar scramjets over the last ten years. [19]

Defined more exactly, a "scramjet" is short for *super- sonic combustion ramjet*. These are essentially "air- breathing" engines, which take oxygen from the atmosphere more similar to the way a jet engine does, but which can nonetheless attain rocket-like speeds. With regard to the differences between these two, rockets, by definition, must carry fuel that already contains oxidants needed for combustion, since they often travel into airless space. A missile, on the other hand, if following a path that remains within Earth's atmosphere, can draw oxygen from the air around it. Thus, to employ language correctly, "anomalous missile" might indeed be a better term for describing unidentified or otherwise strange projectiles, rather than "ghost rocket," although the employment of the latter has been used throughout this essay due to its familiarity in relation to UFO literature.

This debate about missile versus rocket, however, has raised issues pertaining to technical problems for the creation of modern hypersonic aircraft, due to the complexities that come with building projectiles aimed at reaching rocket-speeds, while functioning mainly like a missile:

> [R]eaching hypersonic speeds of Mach 5 and above with an air-breathing engine means getting combustion to happen in a stream of supersonic air... This leaves engineers with a big problem: injecting and igniting fuel in a supersonic airstream is like "lighting a match in a hurricane and keeping it lit," says Russell Cummings, a hypersonic-propulsion expert at California Polytechnic State University. [20]

And even aside from the argument over achieving practical hypersonic flight today, how easily would it be to assume that research into aircraft like the X-51 WaveRider and similar scramjets had been taking place in 1992? Even travelling at estimated supersonic speeds, as the crew aboard United Airlines Flight 934 had guessed when they observed a fifty-foot-long "missile" in August of 1992, the craft observed does not match any known aircraft that would have been operating during that period. Nonetheless, could it be that experimental supersonic aircraft were in use at the time, and that they had been the predecessors of unmanned craft like the X-51 we hear about today?

Whatever the case, these early incidents regarding anomalous missile sightings would bring the phenomenon into a new decade, and by the turn of the century, the ongoing presence of mysterious missiles in our airspace would resolve in what was now half a century of "ghost rocket" reports, in addition to a plethora of other unexplained objects documented by different governmental and civilian agencies since the end of World War II. And yet, what were destined to be some of the most demanding and controversial projectile incidents were yet to follow; again, prior to the new millennium, one of the greatest unsolved cases involving the destruction of a commercial airliner would erupt into speculation over acts of terrorism, this time against the United States. While conventional explanations would go on to remove the possibility that militant anti-American groups had been operating with intent to cause widespread fear and destruction, what would remain, though largely unreported, would be more reports of missile and rocket-like projectiles, darting dangerously through the skies along the northeastern coast of the United States.

CHAPTER FOUR

FEAR AND FLARES OVER LONG ISLAND

"This accident, this report, over 50,000 pages, if you take and just look at certain pieces of it, you can move the cause of this accident any way you want. You can take just the radar; you can say it was a missile. You have to take all of the pieces and look at them as a whole."

John Goglia, NTSB Investigator of the TWA Flight 800 Incident, speaking to CNN News in 2013

During the late summer months of 1996, federal agencies in the United States were working with haste to determine the cause of a widely publicized, and highly controversial aircraft incident that had taken place on July 17 off the New York coast. At the time, the official cause of an explosion that claimed TWA Flight 800, a Boeing 747-131 trans-Atlantic passenger plane at approximately 8:30 PM Eastern Time, remained inconclusive. However, legitimate concern had been aroused, based on eyewitness accounts of the blast, which suggested the possibility of a terrorist act. The consensus that unfolded during the first few days of the investigation had led many to believe a missile-like object had been involved, after many claimed to see a projectile-like object moving toward the aircraft as it flew over Long Island.

Flight 800 had been in route to Paris, France from John F. Kennedy International Airport, and had only been airborne for twelve minutes when an anomalous explosion brought the plane down. However, with the passage of many years, a report based on an extensive investigation conducted by the National Transportation Safety Board would indicate that the blast had emanated from the center wing fuel tank, when a flammable fuel and air mixture ignited within. Electrical short circuits outside the tank, aided by general design flaws of the Boeing 747 aircraft that prevented fuel vapor from remaining cool enough to avert combustion, were considered the most likely cause for the ignition. However, despite being asserted as the most likely

cause, the NTSB report noted that this could not be confirmed with absolute certainty. [1]

The initial belief that a missile or other incendiary
device had caused the explosion aboard TWA Flight 800
would prove to be a difficult one for the public mind to let
go of, and even many with background in government
would begin to question whether a cover up of some sort
had occurred. Retired Navy pilot William S. Donaldson
had been one of several outspoken advocates of an
alternative theory for the blast, believing instead the
evidence did indeed point to a shoulder-mounted missile or
other projectile that collided with the plane. Donaldson
would go on to form an organization called the Associated
Retired Aviation Professionals (ARAP), consisting of
former pilots, engineers, and members of government that
would conduct their own investigation into the Flight 800
crash.

An experienced Naval crash investigator, Donaldson,
working alongside his group of retired professionals, as well
as those within the ongoing NTSB investigation, produced
an extensive report on the crash, along with numerous
correspondences addressed to James Hall, then chairman
of the NTSB. [2] According to the website of the ARAP,
information uncovered in early 1999 "shows that TWA
Flight 800 could have been shot down by one or more
shoulder-fired missiles. The FBI was briefed by military
missile experts in the Fall of 1996 that Flight 800 was well
within the range of a shoulder fired missile," and that the
FBI had "conducted a covert dredging operation for stinger

missile parts between November 1996 and April 1997." [3] Donaldson went on to testify before the House Aviation Subcommittee on May 6, 1999, at which time this new information was discussed publicly. However, the ARAP's findings are still considered to fall outside the official line of thought as to the cause of the crash.

As described above, the theory that William S. Donaldson had proposed regarding the TWA Flight 800 crash involved a shoulder-mounted missile being fired at the plane, which according to the ARAP's research would have been close enough to the mainland at the time of the explosion to be considered within striking distance. Interestingly, explosive residue was in fact found on some portions of the plane that were later recovered; however, according to the NTSB analysis, if this had resulted from an explosion that downed the plane, it also should have easily been dissolved after being submerged for 48 hours or more in ocean water, as most of the recovered wreckage had been. This led NTSB investigators to suppose that any such residue found on recovered portions of the aircraft would more likely have been due to later contamination as a result of military personnel involved with the recovery of the wreckage. [4]

Still, perhaps the most curious matter relating to allegations of a conspiracy involving TWA Flight 800 had to do with the witnesses themselves, many of whom stated that they had seen a missile-like object streaking through the sky toward the plane prior to exploding. Paul J. Angelides, a consulting engineer, had been among those who claimed to

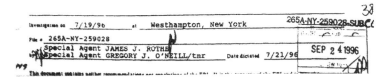

FD-302 (Rev. 3-10-82)

319

- 1 -

FEDERAL BUREAU OF INVESTIGATION

Date of transcription _____7/21/96_____

▬▬▬▬▬ was interviewed at ▬▬▬▬▬
Westhampton, New York. After being advised of the identities of
the interviewing agents and the nature of the interview, ▬▬▬▬▬
provided the following information:

On the evening of July 17, 1996, ▬▬▬▬▬ was at the
WESTHAMPTON YACHT SQUADRON on an outside covered porch. Between
8:30 and 8:45 p.m., ▬▬▬▬▬ saw what she initially thought was a
boat flare. She saw the flare when it was already at a midpoint
in the sky. She was facing south overlooking Moriches Bay and
Dune Road. As ▬▬▬▬▬ faced south, she estimated that the flare
would have been at about 11:00. She did not see where the flare
originated from, but thought that it was as close as the bay.

The flare continued ascending for about three seconds,
but ▬▬▬▬▬ took her eyes off of it as she looked or a boat in
the bay which she thought may have sent up the flare. The flare
was red-orange in color with white in the middle, elongated in
shape like a baseball bat, but more squat. ▬▬▬▬▬ did not see
any smoke or anything trailing the flare, but advised that she
was focusing on the light. The light seemed to be moving away
from her, as if further south.

As the flare ascended, it suddenly turned a deeper
orange, and got larger, but not exactly round in shape. ▬▬▬▬▬
did not hear anything at that point. Slowly, the entire body of
fire descended and became more misformed in shape. ▬▬▬▬▬
described the shape as being like a "pulled tooth". ▬▬▬▬▬
expected the fire to descend into the bay, but lost sight of it
as it descended much farther south beyond Dune Road. There was a
smoke trail following the fire mass as it descended downward.

▬▬▬▬▬ resides at ▬▬▬▬▬ Remsenburg, New
York. ▬▬▬▬▬ She advised that her boyfriend, ▬▬▬▬▬
▬▬▬▬ also saw it. He can be reached at the same number.

Investigation on 7/19/96 at Westhampton, New York		265A-NY-259028-SUBC(
File # 265A-NY-259028		
Special Agent JAMES J. ROTHE		
Special Agent GREGORY J. O'NEILL/tmr Date dictated 7/21/96		SEP 2 4 1996

38

This document contains neither recommendations nor conclusions of the FBI. It is the property of the FBI and is ...

*One of many FBI witness statement summaries recounting a missile-
like object seen streaking toward TWA Flight 800 the night of the fatal
crash. An NTSB investigation would later determine reports of a flare-
like object were consistent with the path Flight 800 had taken. ©
Federal Bureau of Investigation 2007. Source: Wikipedia.*

see such an object travelling along an upward trajectory. Angelides had been staying in a beach house along the coast nearby on the night of the incident, when he observed a red, "phosphorescent object" over the ocean:

> The object was quite high in the sky... and was slightly to the west and off shore of my position. At first it appeared to be moving slowly, almost hanging and descending, and was leaving a white smoke trail. The smoke trail was short and the top of the smoke trail has a clockwise, parabolic shaped hook towards the shore. My first reaction was that I was looking at a marine distress flare which had been fired from a boat. [5]

Shortly afterward, Angelides observed the explosions of TWA Flight 800, and continued to watch what he described as "chaos" unfolding out over the ocean. Later, when questioned by the FBI, he had been asked specifically about the "missile" he had seen. Upon contacting them again the following year to reaffirm what he had witnessed the night of the crash, he expressed again his feeling that a projectile could have been involved, for which the agency expressed little interest at that time. [6]

Journalist Reed Irvine, writing in his weekly news column in August of 1998, discussed more than 400 witnesses who had apparently been interviewed, as reported by the *New York Post*. Like Paul Angelides, many thought they had seen a missile, although only a handful of those interviewed were even mentioned as "notable witnesses" within the NTSB report that was eventually published. Out of the 400 or so witnesses that existed, Irvine wrote that no less than 115 had claimed to see an object that seemed to follow an ascending path as it traveled:

> Even if all those people were accurate in their observations only one time out of ten, the probability that they had seen something ascending would be virtually 100 percent, but the FBI and NTSB dismissed their testimony as invalid. Their justification for this decision was that visibility at the time of the explosion was 6.95 miles and they said "the closest eyewitness to the disaster was over 10 miles away." That is false. The crash site was seven nautical miles south of the barrier island, where many of the eyewitnesses were located. There were eyewitnesses on boats who were even closer. One was an FBI agent, George Gabriel, who reported that a missile had brought down the plane. Most of them saw a missile that was launched from a point estimated to be only a mile or two offshore, and some of them both saw it and heard its sonic boom. [7]

With more controversial theories afoot regarding the TWA Flight 800 crash, official research into what else could have caused the blast had begun to cover everything from electrostatic research and sulfide-deposit tests, to the rather interesting inclusion of meteorite strike probability. On page 177 of the NTSB report, a short section was devoted to this rather strange possibility; obviously, this still seems to be an attempt to account for the appearances of illuminated objects seen streaking through the evening sky around the time of the explosion. The following is a statistical analysis of data regarding whether any such likelihood that a meteorite could have struck TWA Flight 800 existed, contained within the official NTSB report on the crash:

> During the evenings after the TWA flight 800 accident, many meteorites were observed in the northeastern United States. Therefore, the Safety Board considered the possibility that TWA flight 800 was struck by a meteorite, which then caused the CWT explosion. The Board consulted an expert in the study of meteorites, a professor from the University of Pittsburgh's Department of Geology and Planetary Science, to evaluate the possibility of a meteorite hitting an airplane. According to the professor's testimony, knowing the frequency with which meteorites have struck cars and dwellings over the past several decades, and based on a comparison of estimates of (1) the area of the earth's surface represented by cars and dwellings with (2) the area of the earth's surface represented by airplanes in the air at any given time, he calculated that a meteorite could be

expected to strike an aircraft once every 59,000 to 77,000 years.[8]

While the probability of a meteorite collision does seem rather low based on these statistics, it is nonetheless interesting to note the apparent presence of "many meteorites" that were observed around the time of the crash. With care not to draw a tenuous connection to earlier reports of similar aerial mysteries, it is also well worth pointing out that many of the famous "ghost rocket" reports from decades past had also involved objects resembling meteors, but which were often observed following an ascending or otherwise erratic flight path.

Despite the conflicting opinions regarding the cause of the TWA Flight 800 incident, an official report issued by the Naval Air Warfare Center, Weapons Division, came to the following conclusions:

No conclusive evidence of missile impacts exists on any of the recovered wreckage of TWA flight 800. No evidence of high-velocity fragment impacts exists, which indicates a live warhead did not detonate within or near the exterior of the aircraft... The possibility that a shoulder-launched missile was launched at TWA flight 800, failed to intercept it, self-destructed in close proximity, and initiated the breakup of the aircraft is highly improbable. [9]

Can the possibility of a missile incident indeed be ruled out completely, and if so, could all the eyewitness testimony be completely discounted as people's imaginations running wild during conditions of poor visibility? Our purpose here for examining one of the most mysterious and deadly incidents in modern aviation history, rather than to advocate a viewpoint favoring conspiracies pertaining to the TWA Flight 800 incident, is to examine credible reports of anomalous missile-like activity in conjunction with the crash. While the missile theory as a causal factor in relation to this incident has by now been officially discounted, agencies including the CIA and FBI had initially felt there was a strong possibility that a missile had been involved, as expressed in a memo later made available at the CIA's website:

> FBI and National Transportation Safety Board (NTSB) investigators almost immediately focused on three possible causes: a bomb, a missile, or a mechanical failure. The missile theory seemed particularly plausible because of reports from dozens of eyewitnesses in the Long Island area who, on the evening of 17 July, recalled seeing something resembling a flare or firework ascend and culminate in an explosion.[10]

Granted, this opinion would not remain a consensus view among the intelligence agencies throughout their inquiry, and today, the generally accepted cause for the destruction of TWA Flight 800, stated at the outset of this chapter, does not involve an anomalous missile impact. This conclusion is based on a preponderance of scientific data that has emerged that instead appears to indicate some technical anomaly on board the craft, which was responsible for the strange and tragic incident that claimed the lives of

Reconstructing the TWA Flight 800 wreckage Photo by Jan Staller, © NTSB 2009. Source: Wikipedia.

all those who were on board the plane at the time.

Though history may argue the TWA Flight 800 crash had been a tragic, but essentially open-and-shut case, this conclusion had never seemed to be enough to silence a number of skeptics who think otherwise. In fact, at the time of publication of this book, a new documentary purporting to have obtained conclusive evidence of a blast originating outside the aircraft, said to have been corroborated with radar data, was slated for release while alleging that the missile theory could indeed still hold merit. But whether or not an external blast had been the reality behind the tragic incident, a careful examination of available data points to an equally astounding new facet to the mystery: that there were, in fact, other reports of projectiles seen in the very same area over Long Island, spanning the months before and after the TWA Flight 800 incident. At present, no reasonable explanation seems to exist for these sightings, or has even been acknowledged, despite the severity of their implications.

ONE GREEN MISSILE, MULTIPLE WITNESSES

Less than a year before the Flight 800 incident, the crew of two separate commercial flights, Lufthansa Flight 405 and British Airways 226, observed a strange, brightly lit object as it flew past them on the night of November 17, 1995 over Long Island, New York. The two airliners were flying 30-40 miles apart at the time, and at approximately 10:20 PM EST personnel aboard both craft observed what appeared to be a greenish projectile flying 3000 feet above and to the left of them. The incident would lead FAA officials and crewmembers that witnessed the object to speculate about its nature, ranging from the possibility of some military aircraft (the location of the sighting was just north of an airspace used for military operations, according to FAA records), to a possible meteorite. Peter Davenport, director of the National UFO Reporting Center (nuforc.org) compiled additional information about the incident, which was also recreated and included in an animation made available at the ARAP website. [11] According to Davenport, the craft was described as, "an object with a bright light on the front and a green trail," and its duration in the sky seemed to rule out meteors as a possible cause. Furthermore, while observed by multiple witnesses between Lufthansa Flight 405 and British Airways Flight 226, the object still managed to evade detection by radar at the Air Route Traffic Control Center at nearby Nashua, New Hampshire. [12]

Davenport also managed to obtain text of the radio communications between the aforementioned Boston ATC and both Lufthansa 405, referred to as "Heavy" in parts of the transcript, as well as the British Airways flight, which operated under the "Speedbird" handle. Below is the transcript of that communication from November 17, 1995, where the object is described during communication between the two flights leaving JFK International Airport and Boston ATC:

LUFT: Uh, Boston, Lufthansa 405/Heavy.

FAA: Lufthansa 405, go ahead.

LUFT: Uh, we just passed traffic on the left wing, uh, about 2,000 to 3,000 feet above us. What traffic was it?

FAA: Is this Lufthansa 405?

LUFT: Affirmative, Lufthansa 405. We had opposite traffic on the left wing. Can you confirm this?

FAA: Lufthansa 405, negative. I show no traffic in your area within, uh, 20 or 30 miles.

LUFT: It should be now on our tail, about 10 miles... We passed it just one minute ago, and it was looking strange.

BRIT: Speed Bird 226 confirms that. It was just above us on our left-hand side about 3 minutes ago.

FAA: What altitude does it appear to be at, Lufthansa 405?

LUFT: It was only 2 or 3 thousand feet above us. We are now passing (Flight) Level 260. That's confirmed, or not? Lufthansa.

FAA: Lufthansa 405, roger.

BRIT: Speed Bird 226, we confirm that. We had something go past us about two, well... about one to two thousand feet above on the left hand side.

Uh, looked like a green trail on it, and a very bright light on the front of it. We assumed it was an opposite traffic.

FAA: Speed Bird 226, roger that.

LUFT: (Garbled)..Lufthansa 405/Heavy. We are right now about 26 miles east of "Hotel Tango Oscar (Hampton??)." And the Speed Bird is now ahead, or behind us (or where)?

FAA: Lufthansa 405, the Speed Bird is in your 12:00 o'clock, and about 30 miles, 40 miles.

LUFT: That was not our traffic. Lufthansa 405 Heavy.

FAA: Lufthansa 405, roger. And the heading of the traffic, was it the same direction, or opposite direction?

LUFT: Exactly opposite. Lufthansa 405/Heavy.

FAA: Roger. Did it pass off your right side?

LUFT: Uh, left side.

FAA: Roger.

BRIT: Yea, Speed Bird 226 confirms that. We saw the same thing. It certainly looked like an aircraft initially, but it may not have been one.

LUFT: (We can't tell then??) It was looking very strange, with a long, uh, light, in the tail.

BRIT: Yea, a big bright white light on the front, and a greenish tail coming out the back.

LUFT: Can you confirm this, Lufthansa 405/Heavy.

FAA: OK, Lufthansa 405, Speed Bird 226. Thanks, we'll look into it.

??? (Garbled transmissions)

FAA: Speed Bird 226, did it go over...did it go overhead. The traffic go overhead you, or was it below you?

BRIT: It was overhead and off to the left, much the same as ((garbled)). It actually looked about...opposite traffic, 2000 feet above. That's what it initially looked like. But then it did have a very strong trail to it...a vapor trail, which looked more like smoke. And the light on the front was very, very bright, and as it went past us, it seemed to (just?) disappear and (went) 5 miles behind us.

FAA: Speed Bird, 226, roger. Were you level at 29 at that time?

BRIT: Yea, affirmative.

FAA: Roger. Lufthansa 405, how far off to your side did that pass, the traffic pass?

LUFT: It was pretty close, and like Speed Bird said, it looked like (four??) or three thousand feet above on the left wing, just one mile and, uh, on opposite track... It doesn't have, ...it didn't have any uh, lights...(normal) lights, beacon lights, or red or green lights. Only a white light in the front, and with a long green light. It looked like a U-F-O.

FAA: Lufthansa 405, roger that. Like I said, we had nothing flying in the area. You are just north of a military operating area, but the traffic shouldn't have varied out that far out,...out of the area.

LUFT: Must have been a military. Lufthansa 405/Heavy.

FAA: Roger. Giant Killer, (garbled) 59.

GK: Giant Killer.

FAA: Hey, you got anything flying out in the area?

GK: Negative, (105 is??) turned over. 0300.

FAA: Well, I just received a couple of UFO reports.

GK: Oh, is that right?

FAA? Yea, I had a couple of guys that reported lights, just moved all over their heads. I have no traffic whatsoever in the area. They said it passed within a mile of them, like at 2-3 thousand feet above them, opposite direction. (Garbled) green trail out the back.

GK: It could have been a meteor, or something.

FAA: (Garbled--Yea, it could have been that... it passed within a mile of them.)

GK: Who reported that?

FAA: Well, I got Speed Bird and Lufthansa.

GK: No, we don't have any aircraft out there.

FAA: OK. [13]

MORE MYSTERY MISSILES OVER LONG ISLAND

Another incident involving a missile-like object took place the following year on the night of June 26, 1996 at 10:29 PM, which involved TWA Flight 848, en route to Rome after leaving JFK International Airport. As Flight 848 passed just south of Shinnecock Inlet on Long Island, the U.S. Coast Guard began receiving a number of reports of what looked like "bright flares" that were being launched into the sky, within twenty miles of the aircraft. None of these objects, which were apparently observed travelling upward from the ground, were seen by crewmembers aboard Flight 848. [14]

Similar reports involving these strange illuminated projectiles continued even after the fatal TWA Flight 800 incident. On November 16, 1996 at 9:25 PM, an incident occurred which involved an object that was observed, yet again, near the vicinity of Long Island by the crew of Pakistan International Airlines Flight 712. An orange, illuminated object was observed by the plane's copilot as it passed from left to right approximately 3-4 miles ahead of Flight 712, prompting Captain W. Shah to contact Boston ATC and verify whether any military operations were underway at the time. Officials in Boston did manage to confirm a pair of anomalous objects in the vicinity on their radar.

According to witnesses, the object apparently rose upward from the direction of Long Island Sound, ascending on almost perfect vertical trajectory, and while the Pakistani crew had only reported seeing the initial flash of light, a TWA craft flying behind them reported that they witnessed the object as it flew out of the inlet just below and ahead of them. The incident was said to have generated enough concern that the TWA crew nearly averted their flight to return back to JFK, but instead requested a path diversion in order to avoid the area where the illuminated ascending object had been seen. [15]

In addition to the TWA and PIA flights involved with the incident, further testimony would emerge later on, as provided by the pilot of Flight 1504 out of Fort Lauderdale, who was en route to Logan International Airport in Boston on the same night in question:

> This evening I flew flight 1504 FLL to BOS. It was an extremely clear night over the Eastern Seaboard. You could see the Connecticut shore-line from Cape May, NJ. We were at FL 330 just east of JFK proceeding direct to PVD. It was about 10:15 PM when an aircraft asked center the following question: were there any fireworks going off in the area. Center replied in the negative, to the best of their best knowledge. The aircraft then reported they had something streak up towards them from the left and pass in front of them and through their altitude. There was silence on the

frequency. I asked center the position of the aircraft reporting the event. Center replied 20nm south of HTO. It was a foreign carrier, but judging by the accent of the pilot, I would say it was Air India or Pakistan Intl. I didn't get a call sign, and to my surprise, center did not ask any more questions. It was a crystal clear night, and we could see the Hamptons from our position. There were no fireworks taking place anywhere. Unless the controller was working both frequencies, the aircraft was at least climbing to or in the high sector. I did a little bit of checking, and found out Air India leaves at 7:30. PM, and Pakistan Intl. leaves at 9:45 PM from Kennedy. It doesn't really matter who it was. Fact is someone reported a streak that came from the ground and to the left of them and passed in front and through their altitude. It was 10:17 when center replied to me that the aircraft was 20nm south of Hampton. Is it merely a coincidence this is close to where TWA 800 blew up, or is something else going on? I don't believe the aircraft was flying inverted and that was a meteor that streaked by their windshield. Again I was amazed at the silence of the controller after the report. This event certainly got our attention. [16]

It is strange indeed that continuous reports of un-identified projectiles would persist, even *after* the TWA Flight 800 incident, but perhaps stranger still that so little official interest in the related cases over Long Island would be given any serious consideration. And yet, the Pakistan International Airlines Flight 712 encounter would not be the last: again on the morning of December 12, 1996, Saudi Arabian Airlines Flight 35 also reported seeing an anomalous aircraft in this area while approaching JFK International Airport. The description detailed a brightly illuminated, greenish object that passed by the plane, which had been visible from the cockpit window. This object was tracked on radar as Flight 35 approached JFK at an altitude of approximately 12,000 feet. [16]

Whether or not the tragic explosion of TWA Flight 800 had been related in any way to the ongoing reports of anomalous missiles seen in the area in the years before and after the incident, such multiple-witness reports did little to ease the concerns of pilots who were flying over Long Island around the time. Had no such other reports existed, perhaps there would have been little question ever raised with regard to the official explanation for the fatal incident that occurred in July of 1996. However, the multitude of reports conveying the presence of rocket or missile-like objects seen in the area, many of which had indeed been observed as they ascended into the sky, makes both the casual explanation of meteor sightings, as well as the easy acceptance of a freak accident that led to the downing of TWA Flight 800, more difficult to accept.

As a final note, in 2013, a team of six investigators that included two NTSB accident investigators, a chief medical examiner, the senior medical forensics examiner, and others were featured in a documentary titled *TWA Flight 800,* which alleged that the FBI had covered up information pertaining to the crash and that, contrary to the consensus explanation of the fuel tank anomaly issued by the NTSB years ago, a missile or other object might indeed have caused the blast. One NTSB Senior Investigator appearing in the film, Hank Hughes, appeared on camera during the documentary, claiming that his own investigation seemed to be under the watch of a second party, who had been carrying out secret visits by night to his quarters for reasons that remained clandestine:

> [My] hangar had been disturbed at night. They set up video surveillance in my hangar, and found that three FBI agents from another office had entered the hangar, for purposes unknown, in the wee hours of the morning. [17]

Revelations such as these do little to ease the concerns of an already skeptical public, who since the night of the TWA Flight 800 crash, have continued to ask whether there could have been an outside force involved with the accident. Were any of the aforementioned rocket incidents, reported in the same timeframe and airspace over Long Island where Flight 800 went down, evidence of the ongoing "ghost rocket" phenomenon in our skies? Furthermore, could it be that in at least one of these cases, an anomalous projectile streaking through our airspace had proven to be deadly?

Chapter Five

Nasa and the New Millennium

"Pilot-sightings, both recent and old, could readily be cited. Not only civilian pilots but dozens of military pilots have sighted wholly unconventional objects defying ready explanation...Thus, the answer to the question, 'Why don't pilots see UFOs?' is, 'They do'."

James McDonald, *Statement on UFOs to the House Subcommittee on Science & Aeronautics, 1968 Symposium on UFOs*

O ne of the greatest hindrances to gathering data about dangerous activity taking place in our skies—and over the Americas in particular—has involved the complications that can accompany the act of reporting anything perceived as being dangerous. Whether an agency may be civilian or governmental, it is safe to say that few would ever invite getting caught up in the bureaucracy of official policy, especially when negative reinforcement may come into play. Hence, so far as being able to compile important regulatory and technical data on perceived threats of any kind, it is quite often the case that one of the would-be-reporter's best allies is the protection that only anonymity can offer.

With regard to collecting safety information about aviation, the necessity for this kind of information is both obvious, and troubling, for those reasons stated previously. Hence, by the late 1950s there had already been some discussion about the benefits that might incur from providing a reporting database for aviation safety concerns that would also ensure individual anonymity. This would be brought into official discussion in 1966, when Bobbie R. Allen, then Director of the Bureau of Safety of the United States Civil Aeronautics Board, had been speaking in Madrid at a wintertime seminar for the international Flight Safety Foundation. In Allen's view, the negative implications of aviation policy enforcement, such as legal liability and disciplinary action, could often hinder the attainment of reliable, and perhaps vital information regarding aviation safety hazards. "In the event that the fear of exposure cannot be overcome by other means," Allen argued, "it might be profitable if we explored a system of incident reporting which would assure a substantial flow of vital information to the computer for processing, and at the same time, would provide some method designed to effectively eliminate the personal aspect of the individual occurrences so that the information derived would be helpful to all and harmful to none." [1]

Once the sort of system that Allen envisioned was finally given serious consideration, it was decided that its effectiveness might be ensured if it were to come under the oversight of NASA, which could serve as an objective agency, but not one that wielded any regulatory power of enforcement. Thus, the Aviation Safety Reporting Program was born, along with its Aviation Safety Reporting System (ASRS), which in 2011 was detailed in Federal Aviation Administration Advisory Circular number 00-46E as follows:

> This advisory circular (AC) describes the Federal Aviation Administration (FAA) Aviation Safety Reporting Program (ASRP) which utilizes the National Aeronautics and Space Administration (NASA) as a third party to receive and process Aviation Safety Reports. This cooperative safety reporting program invites pilots, controllers, Flight Attendants (F/A), maintenance personnel, dispatchers, and other users of the National

Airspace System (NAS), or any other person, to report to NASA actual or potential discrepancies and deficiencies involving the safety of aviation operations. The operations covered by the program include departure, en route, approach, and landing operations and procedures; air traffic control (ATC) procedures and equipment; crew and ATC communications; aircraft cabin operations; aircraft movement on the airport; near midair collisions (NMAC); aircraft maintenance and recordkeeping; and airport conditions or services. The effectiveness of this program in improving safety depends on the free, unrestricted flow of information from the users of the NAS. Based on information obtained from this program, the FAA will take corrective action as necessary to remedy defects or deficiencies in the NAS. The reports may also provide data for improving the current system and planning for a future system. [2]

As an assurance that the information would both ensure anonymity, and also protect those supplying information from falling under any kind of enforcement action, the Code of Federal Regulations § 91.25 further states that:

The Administrator of the FAA will not use reports submitted to the National Aeronautics and Space Administration under the Aviation Safety Reporting Program (or information derived therefrom) in any enforcement action except information concerning accidents or criminal offenses which are wholly excluded from the Program." [3]

By now, a few may be wondering what all this technical information and legalese has to do with the ongoing appearances of anomalous projectiles. In truth, and perhaps with thanks to the privacy assurances that the ASRS has provided, the program outlined above has boasted a number of instances where strange, missile-like objects and other unidentified flying objects have been observed from various commercial and other ranks of aircraft in flight. After being reported to the ASRS, these cases are subsequently made available to the public in an online database that few, in all likelihood, will ever seek to access, as least while looking for information on unidentified flying objects. And yet, a search conducted of the ASRS collections, when employing relevant terminology such as "missile" or "UFO" will return a number of cases indicating not only that such information does in fact exist, but also that it is officially maintained by NASA.

When an incident report is filed, aviation safety analysts within the ASRS, ranging from experienced pilots to air traffic controllers, and with knowledge of both commercial and military flight operations, will analyze each case. In every instance, at least two of these analysts will review the case, aiming to identify any potential aviation hazards the report may entail. In the event that an incident elicits concern, appropriate officials within the FAA or aviation authority are notified, and any causes for the incident are determined. Finally, these observations, along with the original report, are added to the ASRS database. Such reports have been filed since 1988, and continue to be updated regularly up to the present day. [4]

ANONYMOUS REPORTS OF ANOMALOUS PROJECTILES

One of the earliest incidents involving a projectile-like object that was added to the ongoing ASRS database dates back to July of 1988. On descent into Salt Lake City International Airport, a pilot in flight noticed an object at approximately 9500 mean sea level, prompting him to pull the aircraft up and to the right in order to avoid hitting the object. "I couldn't tell if it was an aircraft or a balloon," the observing pilot recounted in his report, "but it was dark blue in color, and bigger than a basketball and smaller than an SMA (aircraft)." At this time, the captain on board advised ATC that a near miss had just occurred, and the controller on duty replied that there hadn't been any visible traffic to report. ASRS investigators obtained supplemental information, which indicated that both captain and copilot had simultaneously seen, "what appeared to be a drop military style tank or a missile." The object appeared to be "two-tone blue, bullet shaped, with one winglet extending from each side." A follow up conversation with the first officer, who had been the principal witness, did not supply any further information of great importance, although the witness "did say that he thought it was a balloon, but could not be sure." The incident, which occurred just south of Salt Lake City Airport, could not be connected with any activity at the airport that seemed to account for the strange, missile-shaped object. [5]

Another incident from the ASRS databases occurred in December of 1992, this time detailing a frightening collision with an object that destroyed a portion of the windshield on a small transport plane over Arizona. The pilot had been cruising at an altitude of 9000 feet after leaving Blythe Airport, en route to Sky Harbor International Airport in Phoenix, when the left front windshield "was shattered by an unknown object." The pilot alerted the Air Route Traffic Control Center in Albuquerque, New Mexico, and requested a lower altitude and vectors to the nearest airport. The pilot was issued a lower altitude, but told that 5000 feet would be the lowest he could fly while being directed to Buckeye Municipal Airport. However, upon nearing the emergency landing point at Buckeye, the pilot was now experiencing IMC (instrument meteorological conditions) that prevented him from being able to locate the airport. The pilot continued on toward Sky Harbor, but was advised that weather conditions were creating complications at this destination as well. The pilot had said he was so eager to land at this point that, upon finally spotting Buckeye to his right, he began his descent without ever being cleared for landing, and had not yet declared an emergency. [6] It is unknown what, or how large the object that struck the windshield in this incident may have been, and while the encounter did not involve an object resembling a projectile, there was reasonable cause for belief that a physical collision had taken place nonetheless.

While the Arizona "collision" related here presents a more ambiguous description of some unknown aerial object, many of the later reports would indeed seem to entail sightings of missiles in flight. In August of 1996, an aircraft was flying at cruising altitude near Snow Hill, Maryland, when the flight crew observed what they believed to be a missile or rocket as it climbed vertically, passing their altitude, within a distance of three miles from their location. Communication with ATC did not return any information about the apparent projectile launch, nor did passengers observe any foreign object, since a movie was being shown in the passenger deck, and their shades were drawn over the cabin windows, the report stated. The incident was reported to FAA officials, who were notified promptly by phone afterward. [7]

Perhaps one of the most striking incidents involving a missile-like object reported to the ASRS database would take place within just a few months of the missile over Snow Hill, Maryland. In March of 1997, the flight crew of a DC-9, along with other aircraft in the area, observed a missile as it flew by them over New York. The incident could easily stand alone as a remarkable, multiple witness sighting of a strange, green "ghost rocket"; however, its incredible similarity to the startling incident recounted in the last chapter, regarding a green projectile seen over Long Island by Lufthansa Flight 405 and British Airways 226 on November 17, 1995, makes it nothing short of incredible.

The initial report involved the Captain and First Officer aboard the DC-9, who both watched "a rocket or missile climbing through our altitude off our left wing." The crew watched this object for approximately 30 seconds, as it produced a bluish-white exhaust plume that was reported to have covered a third of the captain's side window. The crew watched the object climb through their altitude, and it continued to ascend before finally leveling off just above them. "The object was moving extremely fast, was highly visible, and was sighted by other aircraft," the officer's report detailed, noting that he had reported the incident to the nearby New York Air Route Traffic Control Center as he witnessed it. "It is a very serious matter," he concluded, "that needs immediate attention. [8]

ASRS investigators found that the object was indeed reported to New York Air Route Traffic Control Center by two other aircraft, one of them identified as a Gulfstream Business Jet Aircraft.

> The actual rocket body was not visible, but the trailing smoke was thick and made the rocket sighting easy to see. The rocket climbed above the reporter's aircraft, then began to level off. Another aircraft at FL330 stated it flew under them so the maximum altitude achieved [by the rocket] seems to be under FL330. There is no airspace in that area that might fire such a device. [The] reporter

never received any other info regarding the sighting. [9]

ASRS investigators, who indicated three Air Carrier craft among the four references they listed, collected secondary data about the incident from the captains of other aircraft that had been in the same vicinity at the time of the sighting. However, supplemental information was apparently obtained from another report on this incident, filed separately under ASRS report number (ACN) 363442. [10] Curiously, a search for this report in the ASRS database brings forth no results, although information from this source is still related in the primary report (ACN 363539). Had multiple reports of the same incident been consolidated into a single "master" report, or does this indicate that another report on this incident had actually gone missing from the ASRS database?

In the secondary info obtained during follow-up calls by ASRS investigators, corroboration with one of the flight crews observing this strange, green missile noted they had observed conventional projectile launches at an earlier time, and that the object they had seen over New York looked identical to a rocket takeoff:

Callback conversation with [the witness] revealed the following info: [The witness] states they were just departing LaGuardia Airport and upon switching frequencies heard the description of a missile launch. The other crew indicated they had seen missiles launched in Las Vegas and this looked just like it. [The witness] and First Officer did indicate that the bright light had a tail, which shortly extinguished but it looked more bright green. [The witness] was not able to tell [the] exact direction of movement but felt it remained the same altitude below them. [11]

Interestingly, those reporting the bright green "rocket" here had also noted observing the Hale Bopp Comet earlier that same evening, and ruled this out as a source for the object they had seen. In addition to being a very telling case from the ASRS collection, the incident detailed above also shows that the brilliant, green, and potentially deadly "ghost rockets" seen over Long Island the previous year were still very much a concern. To date, no satisfactory explanation for these incidents has been given, despite the troubling fact that the TWA Flight 800 crash occurred during the midst of this rash of "rocket" reports over New York from the same period.

A NEW MILLENNIUM: UFO MISSILES IN THE TWENTY FIRST CENTURY

Among the benefits of the ASRS database is the fact that ongoing reports of strange phenomenon, which occur within the vicinity of various aircraft, continue to be reported and updated here in an official capacity. Thus, some of the most recent reports of rocket-like UFOs can be found using this resource, as well as sites like the National UFO Reporting Center Website (www.nuforc.org).

Another incident contained within the ASRS database, dated February 2001, discusses a very strange encounter where a Boeing 727 narrowly missed colliding with an unidentified aircraft. The synopsis below is based on details from this report, although as with previous instances included within this essay, technical jargon and related terminology may have been replaced so that the details of the report may be understood more easily:

> Flying at FL280, en route from Indianapolis International Airport to Louis Armstrong New Orleans International Airport, we received a Traffic Alert and Collision Avoidance System (TCASII) alert. TCASII alert consisted of a traffic call followed by a descend call. Captain started evasive action by disconnecting the autopilot and beginning descent. Air Traffic Control was notified of the Resolution Advisory. As the descent was initiated the First Officer gained visual contact with the other aircraft. [The] aircraft was off our right side approximately 600 feet above and then it descended through our altitude. Once visual contact was gained altitude deviation stopped, total deviation consisted of 100 feet below assigned. Traffic was reported to Air Traffic Control, but ATC said no traffic was in the area. [12]

At this point, despite the fact that no clear description of this mysterious "traffic" that alerted the crew's Collision Avoidance System is given, the report nonetheless manages to get interesting:

> Air Traffic Control asked if we wanted to file a UFO report. Captain told ATC that it was definitely an aircraft, at which time ATC asked the captain about filing a Near Mid Air Collision (NMAC) report. [13]

So what was the mysterious object reported here to the ASRS? It certainly does not sound like a missile or other projectile, at least in this instance, although the general ambiguity of the descriptions offered in this technical report leave much to the imagination. The only kind of descriptive offering at all, it seems, was the suggestion made by ATC personnel, who asked if the crew would like to "file a UFO report." Whatever the craft had been, the captain decided to follow through with that NMAC report. A similar incident was filed with the ASRS in August of 2007, during which the crew of a Gulfstream G550 business jet responded to repeated warnings from their TCASII alert system, which indicated a mysterious target only a few hundred feet above them. Air Traffic Control could not confirm any traffic in the area nearby, except for other commercial aircraft a few thousand feet below. The onboard equipment was subsequently checked after landing, but no mechanical flaws could be found that would account for the anomalous TCAS warnings. [14]

The next notable ASRS incident from the early 2000's would involve a crewmember aboard an A320 aircraft that observed a missile pass beneath them. The incident occurred in September of 2005, and the A320's crew had been traveling approximately 25 nautical miles east of the airport on Ramata Island in the Solomon Islands. One of the two pilots aboard (who hadn't been operating the plane at the time) managed to catch a fleeting glimpse of a long, tubular object as it passed beneath the plane. At first, he interpreted this to be another aircraft, although he said the craft had no wings. Air Traffic Control could not confirm another aircraft anywhere nearby, and the first officer, who had been operating the craft when the UFO flew beneath them, had been looking away at the time. The pilot's description of the object, however, was very lucid:

> It appeared to be a missile. The object was gray, had a round nose and [was] cylindrical. It appeared to be travelling fairly fast. I did not see any contrail although there was a layer of clouds beneath the object and my line of sight. I thought about it for a minute or so and concluded it looked more like a missile than anything else. [15]

The pilot reported to ATC that he felt the object he observed had been some kind of missile, affirming that it hadn't resembled a bird or a balloon of any kind.

Another incident involving an A320 took place over Sweden in July of 2008, during which an evening flight observed multiple appearances of an unusual, brightly illuminated object, which they observed as it travelled from the southwest. The object became intensely bright, and then faded in intensity again as it moved to the northwest. According to the pilot who witnessed this anomalous display, the cockpit lighting that evening had been dim at the time, and visibility of the night sky had been nearly perfect, with a full moon oriented directly behind them. While some stars were visible at the time, the light of the moon prevented many celestial bodies from being visible. The anomaly the crewmembers had been observing was easy to discern, however, as it flared from dimly lit, to "extremely bright" over the course of just a few seconds. The witness filing the **ASRS** report described having never seen "such an intense, bright, white and silver light in my life." As the object continued to move through the sky, the pilot noted a sharp 45-degree directional change, shortly before fading from view. The object would return, however, repeating the same ghostly aerial dance almost perfectly each time:

> During the next 50 minutes, we experienced almost the exact same scenario four more times. The First Officer witnessed all four of those events... the last one we saw was on descent into [Kristianstad Airport] around 17,000 feet as we entered a cloud. [16]

Another crewmember described the same object as resembling "a very weak looking star" at the outset, which would slowly begin to get brighter at its peak, then dim slowly as it flew off toward the northwest. "I have background in the USAF," the secondary witness told ASRS investigators, "and the closest I could describe this point of light would possibly be similar to an airborne-launched missile." [17]

REPORTS OF INTEREST: NOTABLE CONTEMPORARY NUFORC PROJECTILE INCIDENTS

In addition to the reports of anomalous aerial phenomenon and unidentified aircraft collected by the ASRS, one of the very best resources containing similar information can be found in the aforementioned National UFO Reporting Center (NUFORC), managed by Peter Davenport. Outside the context of UFO studies, some might frown upon the collection of data conducted by this organization, accepting the common, but mistaken interpretation of "UFO" as meaning "alien spacecraft." While this is one view that is maintained regarding the interpretation of exotic instances of aerial phenomenon, it is also a speculative one; but despite lacking hard proof, there is still a preponderance of evidence that there are, at times, unconventional phenomenon that are observed in our skies. Again, the more skeptical reader would be advised here to suspend disbelief, or biases toward one particular

worldview or another, and try to recognize the merit of the
NUFORC based on its ability to gather tremendous
amounts of data, which it makes available to the public for
review.

Presumably, there are a large number of reports in the
NUFORC database that have resulted from simple misidentification of conventional aircraft, natural phenomena,
etc. Some of the stranger cases could possibly relate
information of an extraordinary variety, whatever that may
entail, though it is not within the scope of this essay to
speculate about these, or their underlying cause. There is
also the likelihood that there are a number of incidents in
the NUFORC database that would have to do with what are
clearly earthbound technologies, and those of which the
public has little knowledge. Thus, the serious technologist
might consider not just the reports, but also the NUFORC's
ability to gather information and provide it as a resource.
One does not have to be in search of extraterrestrials in
order to make use of the information this organization
provides.

The NUFORC provides a plethora of reports where
rocket or missile-like objects of unknown origin have
appeared, and even a casual survey of the NUFORC report
listings will turn up more than fifty such incidents spanning
the last few decades. While this number may not appear
significant, one should keep in mind that among the reports
dealing with projectiles or, at very least, cigar shaped or
cylindrical objects that resemble missiles, the majority of the
available reports only span a period from the mid 1990s to

the present, indicating an average of more than fifteen reports every decade. This rough figure, added alongside the reports already covered in the present study, does indicate a significant number of anomalous missile reports over time. Finally, the majority of records kept since the institution of publicly available online databases like the **ASRS** and **NUFORC** document the late 1980s onward. It could be argued that if such organizations had existed in earlier times, and with the ease of access the Internet provides today, we might indeed have a good number of additional projectile sightings spanning the decades between the 1950s through the early 1990s.

Finally, it should also be noted that **UFO** sightings resembling flying manmade projectiles or actual missile launches are routinely checked and cross-referenced by **NUFORC**, in relation to scheduled missile launches from locations such as Vandenberg Air Force Base. Some reports have been conclusively identified in this manner, and notes are added to any database entries indicating such when information about a **UFO** sighting is consistent with a scheduled missile launch or other military operation in that area (for example, in one instance a very detailed projectile report submitted to the **NUFORC** in September of 2001 helped determine the likely cause to be reentry of a Soviet rocket shell, as reported by the U. S. Space Command at Peterson Air Force Base in Colorado Springs [18]).

What follows is a synopsis of a few notable modern sightings of projectile objects reported since 2002 (however, a more complete chronological listing of anomalous missile reports will be included in the appendix section of this book):

OCTOBER 30, 2002: A long, cigar-shaped object was observed traveling at a moderate speed over Potomac, Montana, near a wildlife sanctuary along the Blackfoot River. The craft was fitted with two small fins, was a silvery color, and produced no sound or exhaust as it passed overhead. The general description of the object detailed that it was "almost missile shaped. The object was visible for close to two minutes. [19]

JUNE 30, 2005: Witness standing at the corner of 46th Street and Chicamauga Road in Rossville, Georgia, reports seeing a 30-40 foot long "missile" landing on a ridge to the south. The object was illuminated, and the primary witness, along with his wife, managed to observe this craft from their automobile. The craft resembled a "NASA rocket," and appeared to be emitting sparks from the base as it descended. [20]

NOVEMBER 12, 2008: Two individuals travelling together with two other friends in an automobile describe seeing an object, believed to be a Tomahawk missile, as it passed over them near Randolph, Massachusetts. The primary witness had been in the front passenger seat, and served as a police officer in the Air Force for ten years. The witness and his girlfriend, who was driving at the time, observed the object as it passed from right to left over US Highway 93 moving at "extreme speed." [21]

APRIL 20, 2009: A glowing, cigar-shaped object was observed over Houston, Texas, as it moved through the sky northwest of Houston Intercontinental Airport. The object followed a path described as moving to the east, then downward toward the west. Witnesses were traveling north on JFK Boulevard toward Airport Terminal A, and one of them, a retired member of the US Air Force, expressed concern that they were witnessing a missile attack underway. The witnesses felt that ATC nearby should have been able to observe the craft, and no crashes or other incidents had been reported in the area. [22]

SEPTEMBER 27, 2012: Two rocket-like objects, each leaving white exhaust or contrails, were seen as they passed over Holly Springs, Georgia. The two objects "rose to incredible height" and then appeared to level off and follow the curvature of the Earth, following divergent paths that headed southeast and northwest respectively. These objects were observed "moving at a very high rate of speed," and were visible for approximately four minutes. Witnesses stated that they contacted NASA and nearby Dobbins Reserve Air Force Base by phone, and were unable to obtain further information on the apparent projectiles they had observed. [23]

The reports listed here are, again, merely a sampling of the kinds of data available that suggests how unexplained projectile incidents continue to occur. As previous cases also illustrate, it is clear that many of these objects are seen in close proximity to airports, and are often observed by witnesses who have military experience. Such sightings can often elicit extreme concern or fear, based on the perception that they may be evidence of terrorist activity or other hostile intent. Whatever source (or sources) may exist behind these incidents appears to remain clandestine, and not all instances seem to describe actual missiles or rockets, but instead some variety of aerial technology that only closely resembles a projectile in general shape.

Obviously, some of these reports must be considered as misidentification of natural phenomenon, or even outright hoaxes. But could these more mundane explanations account for all the many and varied reports of "ghost rockets" seen throughout the years, especially considering the preponderance of trained professionals with both commercial and military experience who report seeing such strange objects? The process of determining what, precisely, these reports may indicate quickly becomes daunting, since there are a host of variables that must be considered, ranging from those psychological in nature, to the apparent presence of secret technologies in our midst that beg not only further inquiry, but also boast a surprising amount of complexity, at times.

Rockets and missiles are nothing new to humanity, so far as the kinds of technology we are capable of wielding in the present day. Furthermore, the ongoing development of drone technologies and unmanned aerial vehicles that are often exotic in appearance continues to muddy the waters, at least so far as simple identification of military aircraft, remote-controlled hobby planes, and other conventional explanations. As we continue moving ever forward, expanding our mastery of avionics and other innovative technologies, our skies become more and more populated with the seemingly inexplicable. How many of these craft, if *any*, truly represent something that is extraordinary, and at what point does it become nearly impossible to determine exactly what we are observing? While there is obvious promise to what will be afforded us by the innovations of tomorrow, it remains arguable that the rate of our growth and expansion is quickly outpacing us.

We appear to be mastering more of the world around us with every passing day, and each new innovation. And yet, the more pervasive mysteries of this existence nonetheless boast, at least in a few rare instances, that there could be elements to our world that still elude us, and of which we cannot claim to possess full understanding.

Chapter Six

Conclusions: Firing Beyond the Lunatic Fringe

"Don't say he's hypocritical, but rather that he's apolitical. 'Once the rockets are up, who cares where they come down? That's not my department,' says Wernher von Braun."

Tom Lehrer, comedian and songwriter, 1965

O ne of the most recent unexplained incidents, as of this writing, that caused damage to an aircraft in flight occurred on June 4th, 2013. It involved a collision between Air China flight CA4307 and an unknown object, occurring at an altitude of approximately 26,000 feet. Flight CA4307 was en route to Guangzhou, and had not been airborne for an hour before a mid-air collision with an unknown object occurred, severely denting the front of the craft and damaging the plane's radar radome. *New Express Daily* and other newspapers initially reported that a large bird, which was struck by the aircraft as it gained altitude, had caused the damage. However, upon landing, there was no blood or other evidence present that would be consistent with an animal striking the plane. [1]

In some rare instances, electrical anomalies, mostly due to sudden weather changes, have caused drastic pressure increases or static discharges capable of imploding small areas on the front end of an aircraft. In one instance, the pilot of a 747-400 flying from Heathrow International Airport to Toronto, Canada experienced "a huge bang and flash," followed by instrument failure just after climbing through a front containing snow showers at an altitude of approximately 6000 feet. Despite issues with the onboard weather radar, the 747 continued on and arrived for its scheduled landing at Pearson International Airport. "As we approached the gate," the pilot recounts, "the ramp hands were pointing at the nose. When we got off we saw that the radome was pushed in as if a huge fist had punched it in the nose." The cause was found to be a buildup of pressure resulting from a sudden, rapid heat increase and an expansion of air within the front of the aircraft. [2]

Reporting on the Chinese Airlines incident, researcher Greg Newkirk had been one of many that would issue a dissenting opinion on the bird collision theory:

> There's been a lot of speculation about whether or not a bird could have caused a dent of that size, but according to aircraft control, the collision occurred at around 26,000 feet, an altitude with far too little oxygen for anything to survive unaided. Furthermore, there isn't a drop of blood anywhere near the point of contact, something that occurs in almost every case of plane vs. bird collisions. [3]

In truth, recent studies of the Asian bar-headed goose have indicated that in their migratory flights across the Himalayas, there have been instances where they *must* have flown over Mount Everest, which would require flying at an altitude exceeding 29,035 feet. [4] This, however, is without question the exception to the rule, as it were, and it is not considered normal for fowl to ascend beyond 21,000 feet, and even this would be considered rare.

There were other clues present in the case with Air China flight CA4307, however, which included streaks of paint that the colliding object had apparently left as it smashed into the nose cone of the craft. Newkirk further noted:

There are, however, paint transfer marks, which rules out another popular theory regarding collapsing air pressure in the nose. The plane did hit something, and whatever it was has some new white pinstripes.

Perhaps the plane hit a secret government drone? A wayward piece of falling space junk? A meteor? An unidentified flying object? [5]

Of these theories, perhaps the meteor explanation seems the least likely, although any of the other three possibilities espoused here would seem like worthwhile potentials, especially if paint markings were indeed discovered on the radome of Flight CA4307 upon landing. Altogether, the one thing that appears almost inescapable in this case is the fact that some kind of object collided with the plane, and there appears to be no official conclusion as to what that object was, or even could have been, or what it had been doing flying so dangerously close to the path of a commercial airliner at 26,000 feet.

Arguably, in the majority of cases like these that involve strange unidentified objects moving at high altitudes, there would have to be some kind of physical phenomena under-lying their appearance. Even in the event that these objects, whatever they may be in any instance, have been mis-identified or have more conventional explanations, the preponderance of reports where experienced pilots or other trained observers had been witnesses to this phenomenon seem to indicate there is *something* going on. Even if we were to suppose that only a distinct minority of the cases were being reported accurately, it would still seem that aerial encounters with unidentified flying objects, and many of them resembling projectiles, are surprisingly commonplace.

However, along with the potential for the real existence of such mystery projectiles, drones, aircraft, or whatever else these reports might entail, there is also little question as to the likelihood that misidentification of known objects, or simple misinterpretation of more commonplace circumstances, must account for a number of mystery projectile sightings just as well. Consider the following example: on September 30, 1986 Mrs. Yvonne Westgarth of Edinburgh, Scotland, looked out the front windows of her home and beheld a rather extraordinary sight. A strange, cylindrical shaped object resembling a missile was passing just over the roofs of a group of homes across the street. She called to her husband, who got over to the window in time to observe the same object, which they both agreed had been light colored, with a black band around its center. There had been no wings visible on the craft, and it produced no noise as it flew along.

American physicist William R. Corliss noted of the incident that, "No one else reported seeing the object. A real missile was considered very unlikely. However, the object appeared in the direction of the glide path of the Edinburgh airport, where two aircraft had landed at about the time of the sighting." The Westgarths maintained that the craft they observed had not resembled a plane;

however, one theory that had been proposed involved an "enlarged distorted mirage of a Boeing 757," which would have matched the time and orientation of the aircraft landing nearby. "As in many explanations of UFOs," Corliss noted, "one must decide whether a string of somewhat strained scientific assumptions is preferable to believing that a 'real' UFO was sighted. In this instance, however, probability seems to be on the side of the scientific explanation." [6]

In keeping with this skeptical approach to understanding many of the ghost rocket reports, it is also worth noting here—especially after the chronological survey of reports this book has provided, that involve anomalous missiles spanning the last several decades—that there are obvious cultural motifs that begin to arise as well. If anything, something akin to a "missile" craze almost appears to crop up every decade or so; thus, it is worth considering how ghost rocket flaps might work in relation to the broader UFO subculture itself. Writing at his *Bad UFOs* blog in 2010, skeptic Robert Sheaffer outlined the undeniable connections between the classic ufological studies and the ghost rockets seen in Sweden, paired with the ongoing modern reports of "mystery missiles," the latter of which managed to garner attention by around late 2010:

It has often been suggested that the Swedish "ghost rockets" of 1946, reports of which were carried worldwide, played a role in creating the "flying saucer" excitement that broke out over Kenneth

Arnold's sighting the following year. And thus, in creating the entire UFO scenario. So, what I'm suggesting is that the "ghost rockets" excitement of the present... seems to be a replay of the earlier Swedish excitement. We know from present experience that jet contrails can fool even some very sophisticated people into believing that they are seeing rockets or missiles, and this in a time when contrails are already a very familiar sight. [7]

Indeed, we know that a simple jet contrail that appeared over the southern California coast in November of 2010 managed to fool a number of individuals, including one former Deputy Secretary of Defense and U.S. Ambassador to NATO (refer again to the case of the California "mystery missile" in this book's introduction). There is a distinct possibility that nothing particularly strange is going on with the "mystery projectiles" being reported in a large number of instances, aside from the fact that many average witnesses would not know where to look for more information about what they had seen, such as flight traffic data that is made publicly available. In some cases, it may also be that more skilled or inquisitive civilians *do* know where to look, but are unable to gain access to certain official information about what they had seen; this might include details pertaining to military operations carried out around the time of the sighting. With little doubt, a number of secret operations have been, and will continue to be carried out over the years, that employ well-known projectile technologies. While the majority of these operations are probably disclosed, at least some will remain beyond the veils of silence and secrecy, for a time, either for reasons of national security, or due to other causes that simply do not cater to public interest in the subject.

In some instances, like those having to do with fatal aircraft accidents, it may have been in the best interest of government organizations involved to work to ensure that the full story was kept hidden, in order to prevent backlash and public outcry. After all, nobody particularly likes having to admit when they've made a mistake, and if such a calamity could lead to severe political backlash, or worse, the outbreak of a war, it becomes very easy to see why details pertaining to projectile incidents would be kept quiet.

Missile trail in the sky, or merely a sun dog? © NOAA, circa 1980. Source: Wikipedia.

And of course, all conspiracy theorizing aside, no assessment of the ghost rocket phenomenon would be complete without acknowledgement of the mundane. Often, it may really just be that atmospheric conditions the likes of which caused a peculiar mirage over Edinburgh in 1986, or an illuminated contrail over California in 2010, can mislead the eye into thinking it is actually seeing something far more extraordinary than the simple takeoff or landing of a passenger plane. In those seldom instances where nature intervenes in such an unprecedented way, even the most mundane and everyday occurrences may suddenly become the stuff of our wildest imaginary wanderings.

In spite of the potential for secret military tests, hoaxes, cover-ups, and the occasional misidentification of common things, probability would nonetheless seem to favor there being substance behind at least a minority of the reports of objects involving mystery projectiles. Unlike a number of other UFO reports, this seems far more likely to be the case with stories of ghost rockets and the like, since they resemble manmade objects enough to allow even the staunchest skeptic to suspend disbelief, at least for a time. The sheer fact that these objects resemble known terrestrial technologies, rather than the stereotypical "flying saucers" or other exotic looking "alien" vessels, is in itself rather telling.

But what, precisely, does this similarity to known technologies convey about the more credible cases involving ghost rockets? There are indeed a number of theories as to why certain UFO craft may resemble, or otherwise engage in activities that appear to be of decidedly terrestrial interest. Researcher Robert Hastings has worked for decades gathering reports of UFOs seen hovering over nuclear weapons sites and power facilities, and in some cases, system failures and weapon disablement have occurred in conjunction with the appearance of an unidentified flying object. Many have asserted that this indicates a non-human intelligence, perhaps which seeks to protect humanity from its own destructive potentials. However, playing devil's advocate (though not to exclude any possibilities here, extraterrestrial or otherwise), one could also look at such information—if it is indeed based on credible source data— as being evidence of a technology that is perhaps far more invested in earthly affairs than most would assume. Perhaps this interest in terrestrial happenings is less likely to be evidence of benign space brothers, and instead presents us with some kind of technology that is seemingly of *obvious* earthly origin. According to views held by many die-hard UFO researchers in the field today, for one to suppose anything aside from an extraterrestrial presence in relation to apparent exotic craft in our midst is purely ridiculous; and yet, with no hard proof of alien visitation to our planet, how is this consideration of a secretive terrestrial technology any more absurd? If their actions and behavior were any indication of their origins, even in the most speculative sense, then we would be foolish to deny the obvious fact that some of these craft, according to the research of Robert Hastings and a few others, seem terribly concerned about such things as nuclear proliferation and existential crises on a planetary scale... perhaps nearly as concerned as some of our world leaders and politicians. Logic would dictate, therefore, that the most likely conclusion cannot be so easily considered an extraterrestrial presence, especially when no proof has been offered, to date, that confirms this apparent "extraterrestrial reality" in our midst. Again, with no *proof* of extraterrestrial technology visiting us, the next most likely source of this strange and clandestine technology would have to be right here on Earth. Much the same, the fact that these alleged ghost rockets so closely resemble manmade implements of warfare and supersonic propulsion does, again, seem to betray a few hints as to their origin.

There are a number of cases where objects resembling missiles or rockets in flight do not particularly appear to behave like conventional projectiles or military craft. These cases include the multitude of reports where witnesses have observed projectiles that appeared to operate *similar to* a conventional missile, but which left no exhaust trail whatsoever. Some of the objects also appear to be capable of feats such as hovering, moving silently, and abrupt directional changes that any known manmade projectile would simply be incapable of doing. In these cases, it may be that the witnesses had seen something quite different from a missile, but without any better frame of reference for the object they actually observed, they felt forced to employ whatever language best fit the circumstances. In other words, it seems equally probable that many reports of anomalous missiles and ghost rockets involve neither rockets nor missiles at all, but instead merely objects that, for lack of any better description, bear a strong resemblance to the long, tubular manmade projectiles in use since the late 1940s.

There are, however, deeper levels of thought that might be applied to this concept of objects of unexplained origin, which nonetheless could nearly pass as being known technologies such as manmade projectiles. The idea that the rocket or missile serves a position of symbolic importance, rooted well within the substrata of human consciousness, is of little question. Psychologist Sigmund Freud allocated the rocket amidst his principle symbols of male sexual strength and dominance, and his contemporary Carl Jung, who later provided a sharp dissenting voice within the psychotherapeutic field, had also written extensively on the subject of flying saucers, which he likened to being outward symbolic manifestations of people's inner fears throughout the Cold War years. [10] This, Jung gathered, might be able to explain the international appeal this phenomenon seems to have, as well as its obvious connections to allegations of secret Nazi technologies being whisked away by the two emerging superpowers after the war. However, at times even Jung had been forced to admit that there had almost certainly been a physical component to UFOs, especially when some of these objects could be tracked on radar systems.

Bearing this in mind, Jung's theory that UFOs were a manifestation of people's inner psychological fears pertaining to the Cold War reality becomes awkward, at times, since there seems to be only a peripheral effort made to understand what the significance of a saucer-shaped object might be in the first place, especially in terms of some deeply rooted symbolism harbored within the collective human unconsciousness. In fairness, Jung did touch on this subject at times; however, later on, he also seemed to have come within near strides of endorsing an extraterrestrial hypothesis, much like Hermann Oberth and others at the time had done. If UFOs were to be some kind of psychological manifestation, or perhaps even an offshoot of how the mind itself interprets some other kind of external phenomenon, it might have made more sense if projectiles the likes of rockets, in a similar vein of thought to that espoused by Freud, had been the form this mysterious new phenomenon would "choose" to take. The rocket represents both a symbol of strength, and a messenger of impending terror; if any enigmatic new technology had simply been manifesting in our midst during the war years, and furthermore, had been "borrowing" elements from humanity's psychological frame of reference for its operation, logic might dictate that the projectile-appearance could have served a number of convenient purposes, both practical and functional. How better to instill fear and cause confusion, after all, than to don the very same cloak and dagger that a known enemy is expected to wear?

As we have already begun to explore here, there is the possibility that some anomalous missiles and ghost rockets, rather than having to do with incidents involving stray military projectiles, could represent a form of technology unto themselves. If one were to engage in a bit of speculation along these lines, it could also be presumed that these objects represent a kind of technology that is made possible by borrowing conventional manmade projectile designs for some practical reason, such as mobility, etc. Alternatively, there is the lesser possibility that these objects could represent a technology that bears similarity to known manmade devices for other, more esoteric reasons. Researchers Svahn and Liljegren note in their 1992 essay, "Close Encounters with Unknown Missiles," that there are some instances where the objects in ghost rocket reports are classified as seeming very real in the physical sense, and bearing obvious resemblance to known Earth technologies. However, despite their familiar appearance, their physical behavior may be in a manner that is entirely contrary, causing some researchers of unexplained aerial phenomenon to consider stranger alternative explanations:

[T]here are volumes upon volumes of historic data recording "technological imitations"— "ghostly" or "phantom" appearances in our skies. To name but a few: the airship waves over Poland in 1892, the American continent in 1896-97 and over Europe, New Zealand and South Africa in 1908-1914; the ghost fliers in Canada and Norway 1914-1916 and in Scandinavia 1933-1938; the ghost rockets of 1946; ghost fliers again over west-Sweden in the mid-1970s; the Hudson valley boomerang in the

1980s; the Belgian triangle wave in 1989-91, and so on. Many of these waves have been associated with developing technologies in other parts of the world, but with no positive or definitive correlation made.

After all, are these "technological imitations" a mirror of the human mind? In that case the hallucinations are very much of the collective kind. [11]

The idea of collective hallucinations, or at very least, shared experiences where circumstances observed do not seem to meet the criteria for reality, is a troubling one for the scientifically minded researcher. At times, it is better to withhold judgment altogether, rather than leap to a conclusion that would either favor or seek to dispel one view over another. When presented with the strangest case reports of unidentified flying objects, it is often easy to become polarized in our viewpoints, and seek to "explain" these sorts of occurrences either as something too strange to be of earthly origin, or conversely, too strange to be anything but a mental aberration or hallucination. There hardly seems to be any middle ground anymore, once the technology in question appears to exist apart from our consensus reality.

One such "high strangeness" case was related to me several years ago, where an observer of such apparently inexplicable phenomenon shared the details of an incident he claimed that he and several others experienced in the winter of 2000. A group of observers near Hendersonville, North Carolina, had apparently witnessed a strange rocket-like object as it flew across the evening sky during a late night/early morning sky watch in January of that year. One of the observers, D. Fitzpatrick, recalled the events of that night, which to him, seemed to defy rational explanation, and involved more than just a physical object that resembled a rocket in appearance:

> I realized I was seeing something that was impossible, not even an aspect of my own reality, but rather seemed to be some part of the 'greater collective.' As soon as I verified with other witnesses that said they had seen what I had, the whole idea became even more amazing.
>
> The thing I saw was cigar shaped, 'popped-rivet' looking, sported a long needle nose, and had sparks falling out of the back fins like a B-Grade movie from the 1940s, literally making a joke out of its own propulsion... Whether or not the thing was objective, alien, or something else, it's like what I was seeing was a replay of some cheesy 1940s movie, and should not have been in the sky that night. An illusion of reality, appearing and acting as if it was real and objective.[12]

It may also be worth noting in relation to the case above that the observer had also told me he felt compelled to attend this sky watch after a dream he had, which had seemed to foretell the experience before it actually happened. Situations like this are quite common in UFO literature, where witnesses describe feeling preemptively inclined to look in a particular direction, only to discover an unidentified object hovering there. Other witnesses report "wishing" they could see a UFO, or wondering aloud what it would be like to see such a craft, immediately before a strange looking phenomenon presents itself. The levels of possibility in this regard range from the honestly intended, but perhaps self-deceptive act of "wishful thinking," to the more anomalous potential that some UFO objects are capable of interacting with human consciousness in an indirect fashion. Maybe some aspects of their presumed appearance and operation could even be likened to a reflection, of sorts, produced (or projected) from within the psyche of an individual witness.

Despite our attempts here at exploring a number of possibilities, ranging from the inherently skeptical, to those which employ speculative science and human psychology, the general focus of this essay has been to address the ghost rocket phenomenon as a literal, physical phenomenon, and one that most likely has ties to secret military operations or other programs carried out by official organizations. The reason for secrecy in a majority of cases seems obvious: these technologies may represent something the general public is kept unaware of for reasons of security, or they may, in fact, represent incidents that, if deemed accidents or mishaps, would draw massive criticism if widely reported.

There is, however, a final possibility we have explored to some degree in the passages above, and that is the potential existence of an *unknown* technology, either of clandestine earthly origin, or, though less likely, perhaps one comprised of quantities and forces unknown to humankind. Probability would dictate that the most likely solution involves ongoing secret projectile operations, as well as the occasional mishaps that are steadfastly covered up and silenced for political reasons. However, some of the more exotic sounding "ghost rocket" reports nonetheless beg further questioning, based on their extraordinary nature. We need not assert that an alien technology exists, merely to question whether all these incidents could be so simply explained as misidentifications or hoaxes.

In conclusion, it does seem possible that a range of different varieties of phenomena, whether those mentioned

Image © Department of Defense, 2004. Source: Wikipedia.

here, or perhaps some that we may have failed to consider, all combine to form the apparent presence of ghost rockets, anomalous missiles, and mystery projectiles in our skies. We may not have all the answers to their strange and, at times, enigmatic presence... however, one thing, based on the information we have examined here, seems quite evident: these objects *do exist*, despite the mysteries surrounding their operation and origin, as well as the variety of potential sources for unexplained aerial technologies that may resemble such projectiles. Lastly, these objects, by virtue of their appearance, and their association with numerous strange disasters that have occurred over the last several decades, also represent a potentially concerning phenomenon in our world that neither history, nor most conventional technologies of today, can fully account for.

Perhaps some individual, or maybe an entire group of people involved with various clandestine military operations worldwide, knows the rest of this compelling story. We probably don't have all the facts before us here; but with the pieces we have managed to gather, in many instances a narrative still emerges where very little is left to the imagination. Thus, few would argue that this mystery, whatever its true nature and origin may be, presents us with a sophisticated, and at times a *frightening* technological presence that is seldom sought for study; it also brings us face-to-face with a strange and incredible aspect of reality that is taking place in our skies, for which we cannot claim to possess full understanding.

Appendix

A Chronological Listing of Ghost Rocket Sightings from 1942 to the Present

August 17, 1942: A rocket with a long white tail is seen over Osnabruk, Germany.

January 2, 1944: The pilot and navigator of an RAF Mosquito observed a mysterious "rocket" that followed them while flying over Germany. The craft turned 90 degrees and then moved in alongside them before vanishing.

January 18, 1946: The pilot of an American C-54 transport plane observed a meteor-like object over the French countryside at an altitude of approximately 7000 feet. The object fell from view over the eastern horizon, and reappeared momentarily, ascending in altitude for a short distance before disappearing again.

April 5, 1946: Captain Jack E. Puckett was piloting a C-47 transport plane over Florida when he and his crew had a near collision with a strange, cigar-shaped object producing a sparkling tail as it passed near his plane. The witnesses observed that the object appeared to be lined with portholes along its side.

May 24, 1946: A pair of night watchmen at Landskrona-Pasten, Sweden, observe what they describe as a, "wingless, cigar-shaped body of dimensions of a small airplane, which at regular intervals spurted bunches of sparks from its tail." The craft was at low altitude, and moved no faster than a conventional airplane. The following day, a similar object was seen near Orebro, Sweden.

June 9, 1946: A large brilliant object leaving a long tail behind it was seen moving toward the earth over Sala, Sweden, accompanied by a loud crashing noise.

June 9, 1946: At approximately 10:17 PM, an illuminated object, described as "rocket shaped," was seen travelling over Helsinki, Finland, at an estimated altitude of 1000 feet. The object left a smoke trail as it passed, which illuminated the surrounding sky for nearly ten minutes after the object had disappeared.

July 9, 1946: The July 11 edition of the *Morgon-Tidningen* reported that a cigar-shaped object was observed travelling close to the ground at approximately 2:35 PM local time near Ockelbo, Sweden. The report stated that the craft "tumbled right down against the ground and was gone in a few moments." The same day, an object was seen plunging into Lake Barken. Elsewhere that same afternoon, an object was observed hitting the side of a mountain near Mockjard, Sweden, which produced a blinding light and a burnt odor in the air for fifteen minutes afterward.

July 18, 1946: Witnesses between the locales of Ortviken and Sundsvallsbo, Sweden, observed a large cylindrical flying object passing overhead, moving toward the west. The object altered its course and veered off toward the northwest before it disappeared. Elsewhere, two "missiles" were observed flying together, producing a "whistling sound." They subsequently plunged into Lake Mjosa in Norway.

July 19, 1946: A widely reported incident involving a rocket-shaped object was reported near Lake Kolmjarv, Sweden, at around noon. The object plunged into the lake, and despite a three week search by Swedish military that followed, no debris or other evidence of the object could be found.

Early August, 1946: A meteorologist in Stockholm, Sweden, spotted a bright, torpedo-shaped object on the horizon. It was described as being approximately 90 feet long, and "shining like metal." The craft produced a sparkling blue and green smoke trail.

August 11, 1946: Residents across central Sweden observed a number of blue and white lights passing overhead, traveling toward the north. Several of the objects were observed flying side-by-side, and resembled torpedoes in shape.

August 12, 1946: A strange, cigar-shaped object passed just over the roofs of houses in a Swedish village.

August 24, 1946: A 10-foot-long rocket emitting bright light is observed by two students who were boating on a river as it passed over Sweden in the evening. One of the witnesses claimed that the object illuminated the surrounding area as bright as daylight as it passed directly over them.

September 11, 1946: Los Alamos resident Justin B. Rinaldi observed a small black object passing overhead that produced a whirring sound. The object was shaped like a small missile, and moved with great speed until it collided into a group of trees nearby. A search of the area produced no signs of wreckage.

Mid October 1946: A ball-pointed missile was seen flying into a lake in Southern Sweden. The object crashed into the water and exploded.

October 12, 1947: A handful of witnesses observed an object resembling a V-2 rocket that appeared to be on a collision course for a nearby mountain near Guadalupe, Mexico. The object was emitting light and was blue and silver in color, with its overall shape similar to a cigar. The object produced smoke as it passed.

October 20, 1947: A farmer near Dayton, Ohio reports seeing two cigar shaped objects that left a vapor trail as they flew. The objects were metallic and reflected sunlight as they passed.

February 25, 1948: The London Times reports that tourists in Scandinavia saw rockets at approximately 9:30 AM, moving at an incredible rate of speed.

May 31, 1948: An object was seen near Wilmington, North Carolina, as it sped along near the Cape Fear River. The craft slowed and changed course, moving off toward the east just as it passed over the river.

July 21, 1948: A large, rocket-shaped craft was observed flying over the Netherlands. Several witnesses claimed to observe the craft through broken clouds as it passed over The Hague. There were two rows of windows running along the side of the object.

July 24, 1948: An Eastern Airlines DC-3 piloted by Clarence Chiles and co-pilot John Whitted nearly collided with a large, strange torpedo-shaped object over Alabama. It was early morning, and the object was encountered at an altitude of approximately 5000 feet. The strange craft was approximately 100 feet long, nearly three times the diameter of a B-29 bomber, and produced a reddish exhaust trail. It had two rows of windows along its side, suggesting an upper and lower deck, which appeared to be brightly illuminated from within.

January 1, 1949: A pilot flying over Jackson, Mississippi sees a cigar-shaped object pass in front of his plane at approximately 5 PM local time.

August 31, 1949: The *Los Angeles Daily News* reports on a "sky giant trailing a blue flame exhaust nearly a mile long," seen by a pilot and two passengers at 12:15 AM while traveling 50,000 feet in the air over Mint Canyon, California. The object was also observed traveling over an Air Force Base near Muroc, California.

September 16, 1949: A columnist with the Los Angeles Times gives a dismissive account of an object sighting he received in the mail, described as "a huge blunt nosed bullet."

December 29, 1949: A series of odd vapor trails appear over the cities of Fayettville and Greenwood, North Carolina. Area pilots attempt to pursue exhaust trails made by "an unseen plane." Residents describe a blimp-like object, while a Charlotte-based Weather Bureau spokesman said it was unlikely that the object had been a weather balloon.

February 2, 1950: A "strange missile" was observed as it passed over Tucson, Arizona, which appeared to stop and hover for several seconds. The craft produced a smoke trail as it moved.

February 9, 1950: Five residents of San Leandro, California, along with one Lt. Commander, describe seeing a "thirty foot ice cream cone" flying over the Alameda

Naval Station. The object appeared to be at an altitude of approximately 5000 feet, and left a vapor trail.

June 24, 1950: In a widely reported incident, a rocket-like object was seen flying over Nye County, Nevada in the early evening. Residents in surrounding states also observed the object, which newspapers labeled a "flying saucer."

April 2, 1952: A man and his friend observe a UFO near Lake Meade, Nevada. The object was thought to be very large, silver, and flying at an extremely high altitude. The object was said to resemble, "a B-36 without wings."

Late 1952 (no specific date available): An object similar to a "distress rocket" was seen rising out of Table Bay near Cape Town, South Africa. It rose to a certain altitude, and then fell back into the ocean.

April 28, 1954: Hikers near Sare watched a fast-moving cigar-shaped object moving over the Pyrenees mountains at an altitude of approximately 2,000 meters. It was traveling in the direction of Spain.

April 3-9, 1955: Four green objects resembling meteors are seen between New Mexico and California. The objects, which came to be known as "green fireballs," did not appear to act consistently with known meteors.

February 15, 1956: A USN pilot observes a cigar-shaped brown object on a straight level course while flying one evening near Riverside, California.

July 20, 1958: A pair of bright, white, rocket-shaped objects leaving long, blue vapor trails is witnessed by a US Naval aircraft flying at 8,000 feet just north of Hamar, Norway at 9:24 PM local time. Three members of the US crew observed the objects. Swedish officials also stated that a large fireball had been observed in the northwestern sky that evening, which resembled a rocket in flight.

February 14, 1960: A silver colored object resembling a rocket producing an orange flame was observed near Nome, Alaska. Similar aerial phenomena were later observed at Unalakleet while traveling northwest.

March 16, 1961: A meteorologist observed a multi-colored fireball pass overhead, below the cloud ceiling, while stationed in Antarctica.

March 26, 1962: A missile-like object was observed shortly after 1:30 in the afternoon at Ramstein AFB, Germany. The object was said to most closely resemble a sidewinder missile or a dart target.

June 25, 1962: A group of boys observe a strange object, which appears to be firing missiles or projectiles into the night sky over Tucson, Arizona.

October 23, 1965: Radio announcer James Townsend observed a landed silver, rocket-shaped object while driving on State Highway 27 near Long Prairie, Minnesota. Three strange creatures emerged, positioned themselves in a circle beneath the craft, and then returned before taking off and vanishing.

August 28, 1966: Two young boys observe a pair of missile-like objects flying over their family home.

June 30, 1966: A rocket-like object speeds over suburban Philadelphia near Wayne, Pennsylvania. The observer had been a summer camp attendee at the Valley Forge Military Academy.

May 10, 1967: A group of fishermen report seeing an elongated missile-shaped object with a glowing red ball on each end.

March 24, 1968: Irish Aer Lingus Flight 712 mysteriously crashes into the ocean. Investigation of the crash includes speculation about a possible collision with a missile of unknown origin.

September 14, 1972: Radar operators at the West Palm Beach International Airport detected an unidentified aircraft in the early morning hours, which they tracked for over an hour. At 6 AM EST NORAD was alerted, and two

F-106 fighter jets were scrambled to pursue the object. An FAA watch supervisor, George Morales, obtained a visual using binoculars, and described the object as silvery white and oblong or cigar shaped.

October 31, 1976: An observer claims to have seen a group of rocket-shaped objects passing over a busy neighborhood street in Garland, Texas on Halloween night, 1976.

December 10, 1979: A fireball object resembling a missile appeared over the ocean, and flew inland toward Gray's Harbor, Washington. The object completed a directional turn of 180 degrees before crashing into a forested area near the Elk River. Navy Seals and National Guard were encountered in the area for the two days that followed, which included roadblocks preventing access to the area.

June 27, 1980: Aeroline Itavia Flight 870 mysteriously crashes into the sea. Subsequent investigation of the incident points to a rocket that brought down the plane, along with allegations of a NATO conspiracy carried out by the Italian government.

March 11, 1982: Conspiracy theories regarding a mysterious airplane crash in northern Norway include the testimony of witnesses to a possible collision with a projectile or fighter plane seen in the area.

June 20, 1983: A group of boys witness three rocket-shaped objects passing slowly over the Village of Balderton near Nottinghamshire, United Kingdom.

July 27, 1984: A fireball producing a sparkling tail plunged into the ocean 1000 yards south of Lummi Island, Washington. A plume of water rose approximately 100 feet into the air, and the ocean water had reportedly bubbled as it sank.

December 17, 1984: An Austrailian pilot observes a missile-shaped object while flying near the Australian capital of Canberra.

August 1, 1985: Two employees aboard an at-sea AUTEC vessel observe two rocket-like objects passing overhead during an overnight watch near Andros Island.

August 15, 1985: The pilot of Greek Olympic Airways Flight 132 reports a near collision with a dark-colored "projectile without wings," which passed he and his crew on a horizontal path.

August 18, 1985: Pilot Per Lundqvist was flying a Cessna over rural Sweden with three other pilots on board as passengers when they observed a strange, missile-shaped object following power lines as it flew below them. The craft resembled a missile "with steering fins at the back." The crew attempted to pursue the object, but it evaded them at speeds the Cessna could not match.

September 30, 1986: Yvonne Westgarth and her husband of Edinburgh, Scotland, observed a missile-like object with a black band around its center as it passed through the sky over a group of houses nearby. The object was later determined to have possibly been a mirage produced by atmospheric conditions reflecting a passenger plane as it landed.

June 25, 1987: The captain of Delta Airlines Flight 1083 spotted a beige or brown missile while flying over West Virginia.

May 10, 1988: A missile-shaped object with no wings and producing no sound was observed as it traveled to the southwest over New Haven, Illinois, at approximately 7:40 PM. Shortly afterward, a fighter jet appeared as if in pursuit. The mystery craft bore small fins toward the rear, and had an indentation or a ring near the center. Witnesses said the object had been, "a missile or something else," and was observed as it flew just above a row of trees at high speed.

April 21, 1991: An Italian airliner reports seeing a missile-like object passing over the English Channel. The object was confirmed with radar.

June 1, 1991: Two Britannia Airways pilots observe a missile-like object at an altitude of approximately 8,000 feet near Heathrow Airport.

June 17, 1991: A wingless projectile is seen passing beneath Dan Air Flight DA 4700 on its way from London to Hamburg. A German engineer on board the plane said he watched the object fly above the cloud deck and under the Boeing 737, as it seemed to "oscillate in altitude."

July 15, 1991: The copilot aboard a Britannia Airways Boeing 737 reported a near collision with a "small black lozenge shaped object." The missile-like object was observed moving on radar by ATC nearby.

Mid April 1992: A woman observes what she describes as a "mini jet" as it speeds along over Tijeras Canyon, New Mexico. The craft hovers over her vehicle, and then speeds away. Shortly afterward, she experiences a bizarre, almost dreamlike interaction with the "pilots," before waking up in her car again and observing a streak of light.

August 5, 1992: Pilots aboard United Airlines Flight 934 observe a large projectile-shaped object that reminded them of "the forward fuselage of a Lockheed SR-71— without wings but a tail of sorts." The object was seen approximately 50 miles northeast of George Air Force Base.

July 25, 1995: A woman visiting with her niece and nephew observed a rocket-shaped object streak across the sky, travelling toward the south over Marion, South Dakota. The object was long and light colored, and produced a red tail.

August 30, 1995: A resident of Bakersfield, California describes seeing a brightly lit, reddish object rising in sky to the west. It was said to resemble a rocket.

October 13, 1995: A Tacoma, Washington, woman reports seeing a group of five or more rocket-shaped objects in flight. The objects produced a trail of sparks as they passed overhead.

November 17, 1995: Crews aboard two commercial passenger planes observe a green, missile-like object as it passes over the ocean close to Long Island, New York. The incident is well documented, and has caused speculation due to its occurrence in the same vicinity, and only months prior to the crash of TWA Flight 800 in July of the following year.

May 28, 1996: A man and his son observe a strange cigar-shaped object flying through the evening sky over Baltimore, Maryland. The object is said to resemble a rocket booster.

June 26, 1996: Flight crews aboard planes flying parallel to TWA Flight 848 observed rockets or flares that appeared to fly dangerously close to the plane as it passed over Long Island Sound.

July 17, 1996: TWA Flight 800 is leaving JFK International Airport for France when it suddenly explodes and crashes into the ocean. Of 400 witnesses, more than 100 claim to have observed a missile-like object streaking upward toward the plane just before it crashed. Similar reports of missiles seen over Long Island would appear before and after the July 17 incident. However, according to official studies, the possibility of a projectile impact is not considered a likely cause behind the crash of TWA Flight 800.

November 16, 1996: Crew aboard Pakistan International Airlines Flight 712 observed an orange, illuminated object as it passes within four miles of their aircraft. Boston ATC confirms that two unidentified objects had been traced on their radar.

December 12, 1996: The crew of Saudi Arabian Airlines Flight 35 reports seeing a brightly illuminated, greenish object that passed by the plane, which had been visible from the cockpit window. The object was tracked on radar, passing them at an altitude of approximately 12,000 feet.

December 10, 1998: A college student observes a strange light firing "missiles or rockets" into the night air over the Northern California Bay area near Santa Rosa.

January 18, 1999: A bright light described as resembling a firework or missile, though brighter, is seen near Chicago, Illinois. The object quickly travelled across the sky toward the northeast.

June 9, 1999: An object resembling a ballistic missile is seen travelling over Redondo Beach, California.

August 9, 1999: An object described as a rocket or missile shoots straight up into the sky and then disappears over Phillipsburg, New Jersey.

May 19, 2001: A metallic object resembling a missile is observed flying at high altitude near Palatine, Illinois.

July 23, 2001: A long silver rocket with fins passes over Langlois, Oregon, producing no vapor trail.

September 6, 2001: Several witnesses observe a missile-shaped object flying over a nuclear facility in Waterford, Connecticut. The incident may possibly have been the reentry of a Soviet rocket shell.

September 9, 2001: A married couple observes a missile-shaped object as it passes through the sky near them, upon driving into Angeles National Forest Area near Pyramid Lake, California. Shortly afterward, they describe seeing smoke, and decide to stop in a parking lot to collect themselves. The couple then observes a bright ball of light take off at a high rate of speed.

October 30, 2002: A silver colored, missile-shaped object is observed as it passes slowly over a wildlife sanctuary near Potomac, Montana. The craft had two small sets of fins, but produced no noise or exhaust as it travelled.

November 11, 2002: Three witnesses describe seeing a rocket emitting orange sparks as it passed over Kettle Falls, Washington, at approximately 5:30 in the afternoon.

June 26, 2003: An object resembling a rocket rises upward and passes over a ball field near Fort Myers, Florida.

September 13, 2003: A witness describes seeing a plume of smoke traveling over Manchester, England. The object engaged in right angle directional shifts as the witness observed it flying.

April 26, 2004: A fast moving object with an oblong shape was seen flying at low altitude over Longmont, Colorado at 9 PM.

May 5, 2004: Motorists driving between Biaritz and Madrid notice a rocket passing over the Pyrenees mountains, leaving a comet-like tail.

July 15, 2004: A bright ball of light shoots across the sky, leaving what the witness calls an "electrical tail" behind it. The craft flies straight up into the sky and disappears.

October 30, 2004: An odd looking missile-shaped object was observed at night by a man near Missoula, Montana. The object rose silently off an adjacent hill, and appeared to be covered in yellow metal in the moonlight. There were no lights on the object.

June 30, 2005: A husband and wife describe seeing what looks like a rocket landing on the side of a mountain shortly after 8:30 PM near Rossville, Georgia.

October 31, 2005: A metallic, rocket-shaped object was seen travelling toward the north passing over New Milford, Connecticut in the late afternoon.

January 17, 2006: An object described as long and missile-shaped is seen over Phoenix, Arizona by two high school students.

March 27, 2007: A resident of Livingston, New Jersey, sees an object travelling upward into the sky in the early morning that resembles a rocket, producing flashes of yellow and red. It continued travelling upward and then disappeared.

March 31, 2007: A possible missile launch is observed over a range of mountains near Tucson, Arizona.

September 12, 2007: Flashing "projectiles" are observed over Chillicothe, Ohio, at approximately 10:30 in the evening, remaining visible for fifteen minutes.

February 19, 2008: A rocket-like object was observed as it flew over Mount Pleasant, South Carolina. The craft possessed one blinking light and produced a smoke trail.

November 12, 2008: A group of four individuals observes a possible Tomahawk missile cruising through the sky while driving to Maryland. One of the two primary witnesses had been a former Air Force police officer.

April 19, 2009: A fireball was observed over Hartlepool, England, which was said to resemble a rocket or missile going into orbit.

April 20, 2009: A glowing missile is seen as it passes over north Houston, Texas, near Houston International Airport.

December 17, 2009: A motorist during a drive on a clear afternoon observed what looked like rockets passing over Linden, New Jersey. The objects produced a vapor trail.

January 25, 2010: Locals in Harbour Mille, Newfoundland, describe seeing three large, metallic missiles streaking through the sky at approximately 5 PM. An area resident, Darlene Stewart, took clear photographs of one of the objects, which were believed to be nearly the size of a tractor-trailer.

July 23, 2010: A rocket-like craft was observed as it flew over Willamette Valley, Oregon. The object was silver and very shiny, and left a tail as moved quickly across the sky.

November 2, 2010: A witness describes seeing a rocket-like object streaking through the sky while driving along Cannondale Road near Weston, Connecticut. This object may also have been observed the same day near Coventry, Rhode Island (see below), although data is insufficient to verify the time of this sighting.

November 2, 2010: Two missile-shaped objects are observed by a family near Exit 7 off of 95 South near Coventry, Rhode Island.

November 10, 2010: Several witnesses observe a possible missile launch off the coast of Palos Verdes, California. Three objects, each producing a vapor trail, were seen moving through the sky.

November 19, 2010: An observer near Juneau, Alaska, describes seeing a bright fireball moving through the sky that resembles a missile, travelling to the east and producing a smoke trail.

April 19, 2011: At approximately 11 AM local time, a silvery, metallic object resembling a rocket with no wings was observed flying over Leeds, England. The witness also observed commercial aircraft at the time, and felt certain that pilots in the area would have seen this object on their radar.

June 11, 2011: A missile shaped object with no wings, sound, or vapor trail was observed passing over Franklin, Pennsylvania. The object was observed by several witnesses, and the primary observer described seeing the same object "patrolling" a tree line one week earlier.

August 6, 2011: At 11:05 PM local time, two individuals observed a bright green fireball producing an orange tail traversing the sky. The object completed a 90 degree change in direction, which the witnesses described as a very deliberate flight path.

October 25, 2011: An aircraft resembling a U-2 rocket was observed travelling horizontally over Albuquerque, New Mexico. The object made no sound, and left no vapor trail.

May 13, 2012: A possible military test involving ground or sea missile launches is observed from a distance over San Jose, California. The projectile produced an amber-colored trail.

May 28, 2012: Two rocket-like objects are observed flying straight upward through the air near Weybridge, Vermont. The objects travelled slowly, and moved in an upward fashion one after the other before disappearing from view.

September 15, 2012: An aircraft mechanic in Theresa, New York, describes seeing a white, cigar shaped object for nearly half a minute as it moved quickly across the sky. There were no wings visible, and the object closely resembled a missile.

September 27, 2012: Observers near Holly Springs, Georgia, describe seeing two rockets travelling at great speed in the daylight. Inquiries with NASA and the Air Force yielded no explanations.

October 12, 2012: An aircraft enthusiast describes seeing a rocket fired near an Air Force Base close to

Anchorage, Alaska. The witness describes it as resembling a rocket launch one might observe from Cape Canaveral, but that the object did not resemble anything he had seen before. (See following report of a very similar object reported near Hamilton, Ontario).

October 13, 2012: A rocket-like object is seen moving skyward near Hamilton, Ontario. The witness describes this object as looking just like a rocket launch from Cape Canaveral.

December 15, 2012: A cylindrical object resembling a rocket is seen flying over Buckley Air Force Base near Aurora, Colorado. The craft flew toward the northwest, producing an orange trail as it passed over Gun Club Road.

June 4th, 2013: A strange object collided with Air China Flight CA4307, causing a massive dent on the radome of the aircraft. Subsequent investigation revealed that the likely cause had not been a collision with a bird at 26,000 feet. Some reports also expressed that paint markings may have been visible on Flight CA4307, which suggested a collision with an unknown object.

NOTES

INTRODUCTION

1) Moskowitz, Clara. "Russia admits missile caused UFO." NBC News Online, December 10, 2009. Accessed May 27, 2013. http://www.nbcnews.com/id/34362960/ns/technology_and_science-space/t/russia-admits-missile-caused-ufo-lights/

2) "Mystery Missile Launch Seen off Calif. Coast." CBS News Online, November 9, 2010. Accessed May 27, 2013. http://www.cbsnews.com/2100-201_162-7036716.html

3) Antczak, John. "Missile Over California: Pentagon, NASA Experts Say Mystery Plume Was Plane." Huffington Post, November 11, 2010. Accessed May 27, 2013. http://www.huffingtonpost.com/2010/11/11/missile-over-california-p_n_782239.html

4) Donovan, Vincent. "French missiles or just toy rockets? Mystery deepens in Newfoundland." The Canada Star, January 29, 2010. Accessed June 9, 2013. http://www.thestar.com/news/canada/2010/01/29/french_missiles_or_just_toy_rockets_mystery_deepens_in_newfoundland.html

5) Clark, Jerome. The UFO Book: Encyclopedia of the Extraterrestrial. Visible Ink Press, 1998.

6) McLeod, Keith. "UFO near-miss: Airliner about to land in Glasgow comes within 300ft of colliding with mystery object in sky." Daily Record, May 1, 2013. Accessed May 27, 2013. http://www.dailyrecord.co.uk/news/scottish-news/ufo-near-miss-airliner-land-glasgow-1862995

7) McLeod, Keith. "Scottish UFO mystery: Little Billy loses grip on helium shark then pilots report near miss with blue and silver object." Daily Record, May 2, 2013. Accessed May 27, 2013. http://www.dailyrecord.co.uk/news/weird-news/helium-shark-could-ufo-pilots-1864901

8) Svahn, Clas and Anders Liljegren. "Close Encounters With Unknown Missiles." AFU Newsletter, number 37, Jan. '92 - Dec '93 issue.

CHAPTER ONE

1) Blum, Ralph and Judy Blum. *Beyond Earth: Man's Contact with UFOs.* Bantam Books, 1974.

2) Longden, Sean. *T-Force: The race for Nazi war secrets.* Constable, 2009.

3) Naimark, Norman. *The Russians in Germany.* Harvard University Press, 1995.

4) Maloney, Mack. *UFOs in Wartime.* Berkeley Books, 2011.

5) Corliss, William R. *Mysterious Universe: A Handbook of Astronomical Anomalies.* Sourcebook Project, June 1979.

6) Ibid.

7) Caughey, John and LaRee Caughey. *Los Angeles: Biography of a City.* University of California Press, 1977.

8) Clark, Jerome and Loren Coleman. *The Unidentified.*

9) Farrell, Joseph P. *Saucers, Swastikas and Psyops: The History of a Breakaway Civilization.* Adventures Unlimited Press, 2012.

10) Oberth, Hermann. "Dr. Hermann Oberth Discusses UFOs." *Fate Magazine.* May 1962.

11) Maloney, Mack. *UFOs in Wartime.* Berkeley Books, 2011.

12) Bogart, Charles H. "German Remotely Piloted Bombs." United States Naval Institute Proceedings, November 1976.

13) Maloney, Mack. *UFOs in Wartime.* Berkeley Books, 2011.

14) Ibid.

15) Liljegren, Anders and CLas Svahn. "Ghost Rockets and Phantom Aircraft." From the anthology *Phenomenon: Forty Years of Flying Saucers.* Evans, Hillary and John Spencer (Editors). Avon Books, 1989.

16) Liljegren, Anders. "Project 1946: The Ghost Rocket" Documents Released by the Swedish Defence Staff." AFU Newsletter 28, 1985.

17) Clark, Jerome. *The UFO Book: Encyclopedia of the Extraterrestrial.* Visible Ink Press, 1998.

18) Liljegren, Anders. "Ghost flier mystery still unresolved." AFU Newsletter, Issue 41. Archives for UFO Research, September 2001. http://www.afu.info/newsl41.htm

19) Wangel, Carl-Axel. *Sveriges militära beredskap 1939-1945* (Swedish language). Militärhistoriska Förlaget (publisher). Stockholm, 1982.

20) Sanderson, Ivan T. *Invisible Residents.* Adventures Unlimited Press, 2005.

CHAPTER TWO

1)   "Two Local Residents Report Observing 'Mystery Flame' over Northern Skies." Beatty Bulletin. June 30, 1950.

2)   Ibid.

3)   "June 24, 1950 Cal/Nev UFO Newspaper Accounts." Accessed May 30, 2013. http://roswellproof.homestead.com/ufo_calnev_1950_newspapers.html

4)   Campbell, Bob. "Flying Saucer Over Tucson? B-29 Fails to Catch Object." Tucson Daily Citizen. February 2, 1950.

5)   Ibid.

6)   Sanderson, Ivan T. *Invisible Residents.* Adventures Unlimited Press, 2005.

7)   Ibid.

8)   Associated Press statement from Dr. Lincoln LaPaz on 'green fireballs'. Santa Fe New Mexican, January 22, 1953. "The 1953 UFO Chronology. NICAP.org. Accesed June 11, 2013. http://www.nicap.org/waves/1953fullrep.htm

9)   Lorenzen, Coral. "Rocket-Shooting Saucers over Tucson." *Fate Magazine.* October 1962 issue.

10)   Warsitz, Lutz. *The First Jet Pilot: The Story of German Test Pilot Erich Warsitz.* Pen and Sword, England. 2009.

11)   Sighting Report, National UFO Reporting Center. December 8, 2002. Accessed June 1, 2013. http://www.nuforc.org/webreports/026/S26493.html

12)   Sighting Report, National UFO Reporting Center. February 25, 2005. Accessed June 1, 2013. http://www.nuforc.org/webreports/042/S42393.html

13)   Ibid.

14)   Ibid.

15)   Sighting Report, National UFO Reporting Center. Sept. 24, 1998. Accessed June 1, 2013. http://www.nuforc.org/webreports/003/S03917.html

16)   Ibid.

17)   Sighting Report, National UFO Reporting Center. June 13, 2006. Accessed June 3, 2013. http://www.nuforc.org/webreports/050/S50935.html

18)   Clark, Jerome. *The UFO Book: Encyclopedia of the Extraterrestrial.* Visible Ink Press, 1998.

19)   Ibid.

20)   Aviation Safety Network, Accident Database. EI-AOM March 28, 1968. Accessed June 3, 2013. http://aviation-safety.net/database/record.php?id=19680324-0

21)   Ibid.

22)   Ibid.

23)   Mullin, John. "Did British Missile hit Flight 712?" The Guardian. January 10, 1999. Accessed June 3, 2013.
      http://www.guardian.co.uk/world/1999/jan/11/6

24)   Ibid.

25)   Ibid.

26)   Svahn, Clas and Anders Liljegren. "Close Encounters With Unknown Missiles." AFU Newsletter, number 37, Jan. '92 - Dec '93 issue.

27)   Moffatt, Bernard. "Records 'Swept" on AER Lingus Crash". Celtic League, December 31, 2000. Accessed June 3, 2013. http://groups.yahoo.com/group/celtic_league/message/206

28)   Mullin, John. "Did British Missile hit Flight 712?" The Guardian. January 10, 1999. Accessed June 3, 2013.

29)   Siggins, Lorna. "Tuskar Rock crash caused by collision, RAF man." The Irish Times. March 3, 2007. Accessed June 3, 2013. http://www.irishtimes.com/news/tuskar-rock-crash-caused-by-collision-raf-man-1.1293695

Chapter Three

1)   Burr, William. "The 3 A.M. Phone Call: False Warnings of Soviet Missile Attacks during 1979-80 Led to Alert Actions for U.S. Strategic Forces." The National Security Archive, George Washington University. March 1, 2012. Accessed June 3, 2013. http://www.gwu.edu/~nsarchiv/nukevault/ebb371/

2)   Forden, Geoffrey. "False Alarms in the Nuclear Age." NOVA. November 6, 2001. Accessed June 3, 2013. http://www.pbs.org/wgbh/nova/military/nuclear-false-alarms.html

3)   McMahon, Barbara. "The mystery of flight 870." The Guardian. July 21, 2006. Accessed June 3, 2013. http://www.guardian.co.uk/world/2006/jul/21/world dispatch.italy

4)   Ibid.

5)   "Italy reopens probe into 1980 plane crash-media." Reuters, June 22, 2008. Accessed June 3, 2013. http://uk.reuters.com/article/2008/06/22/idUKL226 4892420080622

6)   "Italy's Darkest Night: Part 3 of 3." Historic Wings. Online magazine. June 29, 2012. Accessed June 4, 2013. http://fly.historicwings.com/2012/06/italys-darkest-night-part-3-of-3/

7) Sighting Report, National UFO Reporting Center. June 12, 2007. Accessed June 4, 2013. http://www.nuforc.org/webreports/056/S56501.html

8) Ibid.

9) Ibid.

10) Ibid.

11) Jackson, Harold. "524 killed in worst single air disaster." The Guardian. August 13, 1985. Accessed June 4, 2013. http://www.guardian.co.uk/fromthearchive/story/0,,1017027,00.html

12) Svahn, Clas and Anders Liljegren. "Close Encounters With Unknown Missiles." AFU Newsletter, number 37, Jan. '92 - Dec '93 issue.

13) Ibid.

14) Ibid.

15) Ibid.

16) "Test Flight of MX Missile Successful." United Press International. March 22, 1987. Accessed June 4, 2013. http://articles.latimes.com/1987-0322/local/me-14854_1_missile

17) Svahn, Clas and Anders Liljegren. "Close Encounters With Unknown Missiles." AFU Newsletter, number 37, Jan. '92 - Dec '93 issue.

18) Ibid.

19) Phelps, Mark. "X-51 WaveRider Retired After Mach 5.1 Flight." Flying Magazine. May 7, 2013. Accessed June 5, 2013. http://www.flyingmag.com/news/x-51-waverider-retired-after-mach-51-flight#G4HpILBMAXLB0w4M.99

20) "Speed is the new stealth." The Economist, Technology Quarterly, Q2 2013. June 1, 2013. Accessed June 5, 2013.http://www.economist.com/news/technology-quarterly/21578522-hypersonic-weapons-building-vehicles-fly-five-times-speed-sound

CHAPTER FOUR

1)   National Transportation Safety Board. "In-flight Breakup Over The Atlantic Ocean, Trans World Airlines Flight 800, Boeing 747-131, N93119, Near East Moriches, New York, July 17, 1996. Aircraft." Accident Report NTSB/AAR-00/03. Washington, DC. August 26, 2000. http://www.ntsb.gov/doclib/reports/2000/AAR0003.pdf

2)   Associated Retired Aviation Professionals website. Accessed May 29, 2013. http://www.twa800.com/

3)   Ibid.

4)   National Transportation Safety Board. "In-flight Breakup Over The Atlantic Ocean, Trans World Airlines Flight 800, Boeing 747-131, N93119, Near East Moriches, New York, July 17, 1996. Aircraft." Accident Report NTSB/AAR-00/03. Washington, DC. August 26, 2000. http://www.ntsb.gov/doclib/reports/2000/AAR0003.pdf

5)   Irvine, Reed. "Dissing the TWA Flight 800 Eyewitnesses." *Accuracy in Media.* August 6, 1998. Accessed May 29, 2013. http://www.aim.org/publications/weekly_column/1998/08/06.htm

6)   Ibid.

7)   Ibid.

8)   National Transportation Safety Board. "In-flight Breakup Over The Atlantic Ocean, Trans World Airlines Flight 800, Boeing 747-131, N93119, Near East Moriches, New York, July 17, 1996. Aircraft."

Accident Report NTSB/AAR-00/03. Washington, DC. August 26, 2000. http://www.ntsb.gov/doclib/reports/2000/AAR0003.pdf

9) Ibid.

10) Tauss, Randolph M. "Solving the Mystery of the Missile Sightings: The Crash of TWA Flight 800." Central Intelligence Agency, https://www.cia.gov/offices-of-cia/public-affairs/entertainment-industry-liaison/twaflight.pdf

11) Goddard, Ian. "Animation of Several Missile Sightings." Associated Retired Aviation Professionals website. July 17, 2001. Accessed May 30, 2013. http://twa800.com/images/sightings.gif

12) "Lufthansa 405 / Boc Flight 226." National Investigations Committee on Aerial Phenomenon Website. Category 11 Case Directory, "Sightings From Aircraft." Accessed May 30, 2013. http://www.nicap.org/951117longisland_dir.htm

13) "Text of Radio Communications Between FAA and Two Commercial Aircraft in the Vicinity of Long Island, New York, on November 17, 1995, at 2220 hrs. EST." National Investigations Committee on Aerial Phenomenon Website. Accessed May 30, 2013. http://www.nicap.org/reports/951117 longisland_trans.htm

14) Williscroft, Robert G. *The Chicken Little Agenda: Debunking "Experts'" Lies.* Pelican Publishing, 2006.

15) Hull, Michael N. "Four in a Row and All Ascending." Accessed May 30, 2013. http://www.thehullthread.com/4inrow.htm

16) Ibid.

17) Ross, Brian. "Documentary Alleges TWA Flight 800 Cover-Up." ABC News Online, June 19, 2013. Accessed June 21, 2013. http://abcnews.go.com/

Blotter/documentary-alleges-twa-flight-800-
cover/story?id=19435980#.UcRoAj771TN

CHAPTER FIVE

1)   "NASA Aviation Safety Reporting Program, ASAP,
     and Other VDPs." Website of The Kientzy Law
     Firm, LLC. Accessed June 3, 2013.
     http://kientzylaw.com/practice-areas-3/aviation/nasa-
     aviation-safety-reporting-program/
2)   Advisory Circular 00-46E, U.S. Department of
     Transportation, Federal Aviation Administration.
     December 16, 2011.
     http://www.faa.gov/documentLibrary/media/Advisor
     y_Circular/AC%2000-46E.pdf
3)   "Aviation Safety Reporting Program: Prohibition
     against use of reports for enforcement purposes."
     Code of Federal Regulations, Title 14, Chapter I,
     Subchapter F, Part 91, Subpart A, Section 91.25.
     http://www.law.cornell.edu/cfr/text/14/91.25
4)   ASRS Database Online. "About ASRS Data."
     Accessed June 6, 2013.
     http://asrs.arc.nasa.gov/search/dbol/aboutdata.html
5)   ASRS Database Online. Report Number (ACN)
     82260. Accessed June 6, 2013.
     http://akama.arc.nasa.gov/ASRSDBOnline/Query
     Wizard_Display.aspx?server=ASRSO
6)   ASRS Database Online. Report Number (ACN)
     228127. Accessed June 6, 2013.
     http://akama.arc.nasa.gov/ASRSDBOnline/Query
     Wizard_Display.aspx?server=ASRSO
7)   ASRS Database Online. Report Number (ACN)
     346083. Accessed June 6, 2013.

http://akama.arc.nasa.gov/ASRSDBOnline/Query Wizard_Display.aspx?server=ASRSO

8) ASRS Database Online. Report Number (ACN) 363539. Accessed June 6, 2013. http://akama.arc.nasa.gov/ASRSDBOnline/Query Wizard_Display.aspx?server=ASRSO

9) Ibid.

10) Ibid.

11) Ibid.

12) ASRS Database Online. Report Number (ACN) 500269. Accessed June 6, 2013. http://akama.arc.nasa.gov/ASRSDBOnline/Query Wizard_Display.aspx?server=ASRSO

13) Ibid.

14) ASRS Database Online. Report Number (ACN) 749852. Accessed June 6, 2013. http://akama.arc.nasa.gov/ASRSDBOnline/Query Wizard_Display.aspx?server=ASRSO

15) ASRS Database Online. Report Number (ACN) 671401. Accessed June 6, 2013. http://akama.arc.nasa.gov/ASRSDBOnline/Query Wizard_Display.aspx?server=ASRSO

16) ASRS Database Online. Report Number (ACN) 795848. Accessed June 6, 2013. http://akama.arc.nasa.gov/ASRSDBOnline/Query Wizard_Display.aspx?server=ASRSO

17) Ibid.

18) Sighting Report, National UFO Reporting Center. Sept 6, 2001. Accessed June 3, 2013. http://www.nuforc.org/webreports/019/S19437.html

19) Sighting Report, National UFO Reporting Center. October 30, 2002. Accessed June 3, 2013. http://www.nuforc.org/webreports/025/S25867.html

20)   Sighting Report, National UFO Reporting Center.
       June 30, 2005. Accessed June 3, 2013.
       http://www.nuforc.org/webreports/070/S70793.html

21)   Sighting Report, National UFO Reporting Center.
       November 12, 2008. Accessed June 3, 2013.
       http://www.nuforc.org/webreports/070/S70222.html

22)   Sighting Report, National UFO Reporting Center.
       April 20, 2009. Accessed June 3, 2013.
       http://www.nuforc.org/webreports/069/S69791.html

23)   Sighting Report, National UFO Reporting Center.
       September 27, 2012. Accessed June 3, 2013.
       http://www.nuforc.org/webreports/093/S93112.html

CHAPTER SIX

1)   Hradecky, Simon. "Incident: Air China B752 near
       Chengdu on June 4th 2013, "slightly rearranged
       radome" at FL260." The Aviation Herald. June 4,
       2013. Accessed June 8, 2013.
       http://avherald.com/h?article=463508bb&opt=0

2)   Ibid.

3)   Newkirg, Greg. "E.T. Phone Insurance: Chinese
       Passenger Aircraft Has High Altitude Collision
       With 'Unknown Object'." Who Forted. Website.
       June 8, 2013. Accessed June 8, 2013.
       http://whofortedblog.com/2013/06/08/e-t-phone-
       insurance-chinese-passenger-aircraft-high-altitude-
       collision-unknown-object/

4)   Than, Ker. "Highest Flying Bird Found; Can Scale
       Himalaya." National Geographic News. June 10,
       2011. Accessed June 8, 2013.

http://news.nationalgeographic.com/news/2011/06/1 10610-highest-flying-birds-geese-himalaya-mountains-animals/

5)   Newkirg, Greg. "E.T. Phone Insurance: Chinese Passenger Aircraft Has High Altitude Collision With 'Unknown Object'." Who Forted. Website. June 8, 2013. Accessed June 8, 2013. http://whofortedblog.com/2013/06/08/e-t-phone-insurance-chinese-passenger-aircraft-high-altitude-collision-unknown-object/

6)   Corliss, William R. "Edinburgh UFO a Mirage?" Science Frontiers #56, March-April 1988. Accessed June 10, 2013.http://www.science-frontiers.com/sf056/sf056g11.htm

7)   Sheaffer, Robert. "The Famous 1946 'Ghost Rockets' in Sweden - Were they Contrails?" *Bad UFOs: Skepticism, UFOs, and The Universe - by Robert Sheaffer.* Website. November 15, 2010. Accessed June 10, 2013. http://badufos.blogspot.com/2010/11/famous-1946-ghost-rockets-in-sweden.html

8)   Broad, William J. "North Korea's Performance Anxiety." New York Times, Sunday Edition. May 5, 2012. Accessed June 8, 2013. http://www.nytimes.com/2012/05/06/sunday-review/north-koreas-fizzling-missiles.html?pagewanted=all&_r=0

9)   Ibid.

10) Jung, Carl G. *Flying Saucers: A Modern Myth of Things Seen in the Skies.* Princeton University Press, 1979.

11) Svahn, Clas and Anders Liljegren. "Close Encounters With Unknown Missiles." AFU Newsletter, number 37, Jan. '92 - Dec '93 issue.

12) Hanks, Micah. "Ghostly Receptors: New Perspectives on Ghosts and UFOs." Fate Magazine. Volume 61, No. 2, Issue 694. February 2008.

INDEX

A

Aer Lingus Flight 712, 76, 181

Air China flight CA4307, 153, 154

Allen, Bobbie R., 129, 130

Andros Island, 89, 90, 183

Angelides, Paul J., 107, 109

Associated Retired Aviation Professionals, 106, 107, 116, 206, 207, 219

Atlantic Underwater Test and Evaluation Center, 89, 90, 91, 92, 183

Aviation Safety Reporting Program, 130, 131, 208

Aviation Safety Reporting System, 130, 132, 133, 134, 135, 136, 137, 138, 139, 140, 141, 142, 143, 145, 208, 209

B

B-29, 25, 57, 70, 71, 177, 202

Battle of Los Angeles, 29

Belgium, 43

Brekke, Paal, 13

Britain, 39, 43, 77

British Airways 226, 115, 136

British Ministry of Defense, 80

C

C-47, 25, 173

C-54, 28, 173

California, 13, 14, 15, 56, 57, 101, 158, 160, 178, 179, 180, 186, 188, 189, 193, 194, 199, 200

California Polytechnic State University, 101

Cavanaugh, Charles, 53, 56

Celtic League, 80, 203

Chiles and Whitted Encounter, 71

CIA, 113

Clark, Jerome, 30, 39, 199, 200, 201, 203, 219

Cold War, 9, 31, 83, 86, 98, 163

Coleman, Loren, 30, 39, 200

Colorado UFO Project, 74, 75

Corliss, William R., 28, 29, 156, 157, 200, 211

Cossiga, Francesco, 89

Coyne UFO Incident, 72, 73

D

Davenport, Peter, 7, 63, 115, 116, 143

Davis-Monthan Air Force Base, 57, 62

DC-9, 20, 86, 87, 88, 135, 136

Denmark, 43

E

erratic meteors, 28

extraterrestrial, 13, 31, 34, 36, 37, 45, 66, 161, 164

F

Farrell, Joseph P., 32, 34, 35, 200
Fate Magazine, 32, 34, 37, 61,
    201, 202, 212
FBI, 106, 108, 109, 110, 113,
    126
Federal Aviation Administration,
    96, 115, 116, 117, 118, 119,
    120, 121, 122, 130, 131, 133,
    135, 182, 207, 208
Finland, 39, 43, 174
Flight 132 sighting, 94
Flying Saucer, 55, 202
Freud, Sigmund, 163, 164

G

Germany, 25, 27, 30, 33, 35, 37,
    44, 173, 180, 200
ghost fliers, 42, 165
Gordon, Stan, 96

H

Hastings, Robert, 161
Heinkel He 178, 62
High-Level Nocturnal Lights, 29
Hs-293, 38
Hughes, Hank, 126

J

Japanese Airlines, 92, 93
JFK International Airport, 116,
    122, 125, 187
Jung, Carl Gustav, 163, 164, 211

K

Kolmjarv, Lake, 46, 175
Korean War, 56
Kristianstad Airport, 142

L

LaPaz, Lincoln, 59, 60, 202
Liljegren, Anders, 40, 41, 79, 93,
    94, 165, 200, 201, 203, 205,
    211
Lockheed SR-71, 100, 185
Long Island, 9, 103, 105, 113,
    115, 122, 123, 125, 126, 135,
    138, 186, 187, 207
Lorenzen, Jim and Coral, 61, 202
Lufthansa Flight 405, 115, 136

M

MacDill Air Force Base, 25
Malmberg, Eric, 41
Maloney, Mack, 7, 37, 38, 200,
    201
meteor, 28, 29, 57, 121, 124,
    125, 155, 173
meteorite, 111, 112, 115
Mittelbau-Dora concentration
    camp, 26
Mittelwerk factory, 26
Mount Takamagahara, 93
Muammar Gaddafi, 88

N

NASA, 8, 9, 32, 36, 43, 90, 130,
    132, 146, 147, 194, 199, 208

National Transportation Safety Board, 103, 105, 106, 107, 108, 110, 111, 113, 114, 125, 126, 206, 207

National UFO Reporting Center, 7, 63, 66, 89, 115, 139, 143, 144, 145, 202, 203, 205, 209, 210

NATO, 14, 88, 94, 98, 158, 182

Naval Air Warfare Center, 112

Nazi, 25, 31, 32, 33, 35, 37, 44, 59, 163, 200

Netherlands, 43, 177

New York Air Route Traffic Control Center, 136

Newfoundland, 16, 192, 199

Newkirk, Greg, 154

North Korea, 211

Norway, 13, 39, 43, 54, 86, 165, 175, 180, 182

O

Oberth, Hermann, 31, 32, 33, 34, 35, 36, 37, 164, 201

Operation Backfire, 26

Operation Osoaviakhim, 26

Osaka International Airport, 92

P

Pakistan International Airlines Flight 712, 122, 125, 187

Pascagoula Incident, 74

Peacekeeper, 97

Peenemunde, 31, 39, 59

Peterson Air Force Base, 145

Petrov, Stanislav, 85

Plait, Phillip, 15

Priore, Rosario, 88

Project Aquarius, 96

Project Sign, 73

Puckett, Captain Jack, 25, 26, 70, 71, 173

R

RAF Meteor, 79

RAF Mosquito, 27, 173

RCA Service Company, 89

Reagan, Ronald, 97

RPV, 79

Russia, 18, 43, 45, 59, 85, 86, 199

S

Saint Phelim, 76, 78, 79

Salt Lake City Airport, 134

Sanderson, Ivan T., 46, 57, 58, 59, 201, 202

Scandinavia, 13, 22, 26, 30, 39, 48, 59, 92, 165, 177

Scotland, 19, 156, 184

scramjet, 99, 100

SD2 Stiletto, 80

Serpukhov-15 bunker, 85

Sheaffer, Robert, 157, 211

Sky Harbor International Airport, 134

South Korea, 53

Svahn, Clas, 41, 79, 93, 94, 165, 200, 201, 203, 205, 211

Sweden, 18, 23, 26, 31, 39, 40, 41, 43, 44, 46, 47, 92, 95,

142, 157, 165, 173, 174, 175, 176, 183, 211

Swedish Aviation Historical Society, 42

T

Tongue of the Ocean, 89, 90

Truman, Harry S., 53

Tucson, Arizona, 56, 60, 178, 180, 191, 202

TWA Flight 800, 103, 105, 106, 107, 108, 109, 110, 112, 113, 114, 122, 124, 125, 126, 138, 186, 187, 206, 207

U

U. S. Space Command, 145

UFO, 7, 15, 18, 19, 22, 25, 29, 30, 31, 33, 34, 35, 37, 39, 40, 45, 46, 48, 57, 59, 60, 61, 63, 66, 67, 68, 72, 73, 74, 75, 76, 89, 96, 99, 101, 115, 121, 132, 138, 139, 140, 141, 143, 145, 157, 158, 160, 168, 179,

199, 200, 201, 202, 203, 205, 209, 210, 211, 219

United States, 26, 39, 59, 62, 85, 95, 102, 105, 111, 129, 201

Ustica Massacre, 83, 86, 88, 98

V

V-2 rocket, 18, 26, 37, 39, 43, 176

Vandenberg Air Force Base, 14, 97, 145

Von Braun, Wernher, 26

W

Wangel, Carl-Axel, 44, 201

Westgarth, Yvonne, 156, 184

World War II, 18, 22, 26, 33, 42, 44, 48, 59, 79, 81, 102

X

X-51 WaveRider, 99, 100, 101, 205

FURTHER READING

The following resources may lend further historical and technical information on the Ghost Rocket enigma, along with other data pertaining to missiles and projectiles in a historical context.

American Missiles: The Complete Smithsonian Field
    Guide, by Brian Nicklas

Postwar Air Weapons: 1945-Present (Essential Weapons
    Identification Guides), By Thomas Newdick

"Guided Missiles and UFOs: A Tangle of Fear, 1937-53"
    by Joel Carpenter:
    http://www.project1947.com/gr/grchron1.htm

The Associated Retired Aviation Professionals Website:
    Main Site: http://twa800.com/

    Index of Missile Reports:
    http://twa800.com/missilereports.htm

THE UFO BOOK: Encyclopedia of the Extraterrestrial
    By Jerome Clark

Operation Trojan Horse: The Classic Breakthrough Study
    of UFOs, By John a. Keel

About the Author

MICAH HANKS is a writer and researcher whose work addresses a variety of unexplained phenomena. Over the last decade, his research has taken him into studies of military history, spirituality, sociology and cultural phenomena, humanity's origins, and the prospects of our technological future as a species as influenced by science.

He is the author of a number of books, including *The UFO Singularity*, *Magic, Mysticism and the Molecule*, and *Reynolds Mansion: An Invitation to the Past*. Hanks also writes for several magazines and other publications such as *FATE*, *UFO Magazine*, *The Journal of Anomalous Sciences*, *Intrepid Magazine*, and *New Dawn*. He has also appeared on a number of TV and radio programs, including National Geographic's *Paranatural*, the History Channel's *Guts and Bolts*, CNN Radio, The Jeff Rense Program, and Coast to Coast AM with George Noory.

With nearly a decade in the broadcasting industry, Hanks also hosts *The Micah Hanks Radio Program* on KGRA out of Kansas City, and produces a weekly podcast called *The Gralien Report* that follows his research. You can learn more about his writing and interests at his Websites, gralienreport.com and micahhanks.com.

Hanks lives in the heart of Appalachia near Asheville, North Carolina.

Made in the USA
Lexington, KY
06 August 2014